Sentimental Attachments

Also in the CrossCurrents series

Attending to the Margins
Coming of Age
Coming to Class
Composition, Pedagogy, and the Scholarship of Teaching
Conflicts and Crises in the Composition Classroom—and What Instructors Can Do About Them
The Dissertation and the Discipline
Feminist Empirical Research
Foregrounding Ethical Awareness in Composition and English Studies
Getting Restless
Good Intentions
Grading in the Post-Process Classroom
Gypsy Academics and Mother-Teachers
Kitchen Cooks, Plate Twirlers, and Troubadours
Know and Tell
Latino/a Discourses
Life-Affirming Acts
Miss Grundy Doesn't Teach Here Anymore
Multiple Genres, Multiple Voices
The Mythology of Voice
Outbursts in Academe
The Politics of Writing Centers
The Politics of Writing in the Two-Year College
The Profession of English in the Two-Year College
Race, Rhetoric, and Composition
Resituating Writing
Rhetoric and Ethnicity
A Rhetoric of Pleasure
Textual Orientations
The War Against Grammar
A Way to Move
Writing in an Alien World

Sentimental Attachments

Essays, Creative Nonfiction, and Other Experiments in Composition

JANET CAREY ELDRED

Boynton/Cook Publishers, Inc.
HEINEMANN
Portsmouth, NH

Boynton/Cook Publishers, Inc.
A subsidiary of Reed Elsevier Inc.
361 Hanover Street
Portsmouth, NH 03801–3912
www.boyntoncook.com

Offices and agents throughout the world

© 2005 by Janet Carey Eldred

All rights reserved. No part of this book may be reproduced in any form or by any electronic or mechanical means, including information storage and retrieval systems, without permission in writing from the publisher, except by a reviewer, who may quote brief passages in a review.

The author and publisher wish to thank those who have generously given permission to reprint borrowed material:

"Natural History" by E. B. White, from *Poems and Sketches of E. B. White.* Copyright ©1928 by E. B. White. Reprinted by permission of HarperCollins Publishers, Inc.

Library of Congress Cataloging-in-Publication Data
Eldred, Janet Carey.
Sentimental attachments : essays, creative nonfiction, and other experiments in composition / Janet Carey Eldred.
p. cm.
Includes bibliographical references.
ISBN 0-86709-583-0 (alk. paper)
1. English language—Rhetoric—Study and teaching. 2. Reportage literature—Authorship—Study and teaching (Higher). 3. Prose literature—Authorship—Study and teaching (Higher). 4. Essay—Authorship—Study and teaching (Higher). 5. English teachers—United States—Biography. 6. Report writing—Study and teaching (Higher). 7. Creative writing (Higher education). 8. Eldred, Janet Carey. I. Title.

PE1404.E455 2005
808'.042'071—dc22 2004027528

Editor: Charles Schuster
Production service: Matrix Productions, Merrill Peterson
Production coordinator: Lynne Costa
Cover design: Jenny Jensen Greenleaf
Cover photograph: William A. Carey
Typesetter: Argosy Publishing
Manufacturing: Steve Bernier

Printed in the United States of America on acid-free paper
09 08 07 06 05 VP 1 2 3 4 5

Contents

A Note for Readers

This book was written first and foremost for other writers, particularly for college and high school faculty and their students, but also for writers outside the academy. (I have written the introduction and the conclusion mainly for teachers of writing who share with me an interest in the professional questions that inspired and shaped these pieces. Other readers may want to skip the professional discussions and move directly to the Essays, which begin on page 13.)

The central premise of *Essays, Creative Nonfiction, and Composition* is that some hybrid form of composition can fuse the personal and the academic. *Essays, Creative Nonfiction, and Composition* investigates hybrid forms of composing, using essays that are themselves hybrid attempts, emerging from the benefit of a number of years studying and teaching writing. For this book, I am indebted to the writing projects that have for several decades now enriched composition instruction nationwide and, in particular, to their simple yet sure driving premise, namely that teachers of writing should write themselves. The compositions contained here are not directly about topics related to writing. "Peter Pan," for instance, is about adopting our children from Russia. At first glance, it may seem to have relatively little connection to the field of composition studies. But it's that first glance that I invite fellow teachers to hold, to allow to linger and deepen. I would argue that the compositions in this book are deeply committed—indebted might be a better word—to the field I have worked in, to the field that has defined and shaped my professional and personal life. "Peter Pan," for example, works from and through significant composition issues: How do we compose ourselves? our children? birth mothers and fathers? adoptive parents, adoptees themselves? How do we represent all these individual lives without losing sight of a larger world of people, ideas, places, and histories?

This book is short by design, novella length, I'll say, since there's not a corresponding nonfiction descriptor. I judge the length a virtue, but in drawing on the comparison to the "novella," I feel somewhat like Katherine Anne Porter defending her short story collection *Flowering Judas.* When her would-be British publisher demanded that she add some stories to fill it out, Porter rightly (or righteously) declined, saying "publishers on both sides keep roaring for weight and length, and demanding that I add more stories" (1990 122). A few years later, she reacts to a 1935 reviewer who called her work thin: "Just how thick should it be, I wonder? How much material by pound is considered a just weight?" (1990 133). While I'm not the stylist Porter was (and thus I haven't that defense), the comparison to Porter is apt in another way: like her, I have felt the pressures of life intervening and, like her, I feel the length of my manuscript is "right," in this case for fellow composers, who need, after all, time to compose their own works. Unlike Porter, I have been fortunate to have, in Chuck Schuster, an editor who did not roar for weight and length, but who, instead, created a space in composition publishing for essays, without insisting on an equivalent page measure of traditional scholarship.

Before the pieces contained here were compiled, reshaped, and folded into a new whole, some had individual lives, greatly enriched by mentors, magazine and journal editors, and leaders of writing workshops. I have Jan Eisenhour to thank for her capable leadership of the nonfiction writing group at the Carnegie Center; Jane Brox, for her guidance at the Wesleyan Writers Conference; Philip Lopate for Recursos; and Marcie Hershman for the workshop at the Provincetown Fine Arts Work Center. I am equally indebted to the editors of literary magazines and academic journals who have read and offered feedback on my nonfiction: again, Philip Lopate, who judged for *Literal Latte*; Michael Steinberg, editor of *Fourth Genre*; and Joe Harris who published an essay in *CCC.* Along the way, Marilyn Cooper, Jeanne Gunner, Karl Kageff, and Susan Wadsworth-Booth also provided careful and much valued readings. I am deeply indebted as well to Laura Bennett, who took her keen editing eye to the penultimate draft of this manuscript.

In 1987, I left Champaign-Urbana with my Ph.D. almost finished to join the faculty at the University of Kentucky, but Champaign-Urbana remains home to me, in large part because of the support and friendship of people there, a short five-hour drive away: Dennis Baron, Peter Garrett, Gail Hawisher, Jim Hurt, Bob Parker, Rick Powers, and Zohreh Sullivan. At the University of Kentucky, several administrators have supported and encouraged this work: Greg Waller and Ellen Rosenman, during their terms as chair of English; Richard Greissman during his tenure as Assistant Dean of the College of Arts and Sciences; Steve Hoch, the current Dean of Arts and Sciences; Phil Kraemer, the Associate Provost for Undergraduate Studies; and Provost Mike Nietzel. I am grateful to have been at the University of Kentucky during the height of collegial times, enjoying the company and friendship of Julie Barbour, Dale Bauer, Virginia Blum, Susan Bordo, Anna Bosch, Nikki Finney, James Baker Hall, Gordon Hutner, Kathi Kern, Michel Rivkin-Fish, Peter Mortensen, Cindy Ruder, Dana Nelson, Gurney Norman, Ellen Rosenman, Steve Weisenburger, Art Wrobel, and Jane Vance, all of whom at some point read (or heard too much about) fragments of this work. I miss those colleagues who have since moved from Lexington, although I'm comforted that Mortensen and Bauer and Hutner found their ways to my Champaign-Urbana cornfields. Finally, I have also been fortunate to receive the support and advice of colleagues from other campuses, particularly Lynn Bloom, Lester Faigley, Anne Ruggles Gere, Min-Zhan Lu, Tom Recchio, Kate Ronald, Morris Young, and many Advanced Placement colleagues, including Bim Angst, Mark DeFoe, Marilyn Elkins, David Joliffe, and Karen Nulton, who have listened to fragments during flash readings and offered words of encouragement.

For this book more than any other work I've done, I'm indebted to my family, close and extended—Rick, Lex, Sash, Pop, the Eldred and Muir-Machado clans—and to a group of close friends, including Dee Snow, a scientist who reads more and with more enthusiasm than any person I know; Nancy Coveney, who continued to see the perfection in my newly adopted son even after he bit her; and Teresa Mangum, who reads everything for me again and again and knows me at least as well as I know myself, arguably even better.

Versions of these essays were published in the following venues: "Peter Pan" as "Children At All Costs," 1998, *Literal Latte* 4 (5): 8–12; "Modern Fidelity," 2001, *Fourth Genre* 3 (2): 55–69; "'Just What the Muscles

Grope For,'" 2002, *Fourth Genre* 4 (2): 169–73; and "Daughters of the University," 1999, as an untitled fragment in *Comp Tales: An Introduction to College Composition Through Its Stories*, ed. Richard H. Haswell and Min-Zhan Lu, Addison-Wesley. This work was supported by two enrichment grants from the Kentucky Foundation for Women.

Introduction

New Directions, or Composition's Formal Possibilities

Oh how that name befits my composition.

—Shakespeare, *Richard II*

First-year college students certainly know what composition classes are, yet the word "composition" has become something of a Rorschach test. In music, there's still a sense of a thing called a composition. But when it comes to writing, composition as a term functions synecdochically, by which I mean, of course, that one related part is always made to stand in suggestively for the whole. By "composition," some people mean grammar. Some mean argument. Some mean essays. Some mean personal narratives. Some quite frankly mean that horrible stuff they are required to write in freshman composition courses or that horrible stuff they are required to grade. This has both troubled and amused me. One of my favorite party games is this: When people ask what I do, I tell them that I teach and write. "What subject?" they ask. "Composition," I answer. Then a variety of responses follow. Inevitably, the speaker begins with the "What an important job you have"/"Writing is so important"/"And kids nowadays can't write" response. Then they start to fill in what *they* think composition is, and grammar is usually pretty high up. Still, composition as a teaching subject is pretty easy for listeners to wrap themselves around. Imagine their surprise when I also tell them that I *write* essays—

and compositions. "So you write novels?" They're asking a significant question: what, exactly, is written composition?

This book consists of experiments in composition. I do not mean to suggest that I have pushed composition to its formal limits; in fact, this particular group of compositions evinces my deep roots in the personal essay and might best be seen as something called an "essay cycle." The cycle begins with my own story of late-twentieth-century motherhood, a coming-into-motherhood story of infertility and adoption. But that is only its starting point. What slowly unfold are stories of how we—postmodern academics—create and re-create family as we find ourselves far flung and unraveling from traditional fabrics. The cycle covers, I believe, serious intellectual territory, but it does so by grounding discussions in female lived experience: my own, my mother's, my grandmother's, and the imagined lived experience of the biological mothers of my children, who were adopted from a Russian orphanage in 1995 and 1996. While the composition "Modern Fidelity" directly addresses the question of sentiment—that bugaboo female writers especially must face—each of the compositions confronts the modern suspicion of female sentiment and challenges another form of sentiment infusing a specific modern legacy: a faith in irony, an enshrining of written art, an apotheosizing of authorship, a distancing of art from life.

In *Art and Answerability*, M. M. Bakhtin (1990) briefly explains the necessity of "answering," of linking life with art:

> The artist and the human being are naively, most often mechanically, united in one person; the human being leaves "the fretful cares of everyday life" and enters for a time the realm of creative activity as another world, a world of "inspiration, sweet sounds, and prayers." And what is the result? Art is too self-confident, audaciously self-confident, and too high-flown, for it is in no way bound to answer for life. And, of course, life has no hope of ever catching up with art of this kind. "That's too exalted for us"—says life. "That's art, after all! All we've got is the humble prose of living."
>
> . . . For it is easier to create without answering for life, and easier to live without any consideration for art. (1–2)

The compositions herein reflect "the humble prose of living" but also answer the demands of art. They build on one of the most intriguing promises of the essay form, "the possibility of realizing," as Thomas Recchio (1994) puts it, "the potential interanimation of life and language, of one's person and one's work" (224). We are, as we proceed into the twenty-first century, becoming accustomed to such efforts. Whether we're considering the so-called personal turn in academic writing or the growing niche in the publishing market for memoir, we're traveling outside the traditional, fairly stable, mapped genres of poetry, fiction, drama, and scholarship. Suddenly, scholars are doing what creative writers and journalists do, and creative writers and journalists are increasingly making themselves the subjects of their work. Not everyone finds the move (a fad?) either aesthetically pleasing or academically convincing. *It's different,* goes the refrain, *but is it good?* Consider this outraged digression from *New Yorker* critic Anthony Lane (2003), writing about the "confessional" poet Robert Lowell:

> Lowell, one suspects, would have been appalled by the recent growth in the self-revelation industry, whose principal criteria, whether on TV or in memoirs of abused childhoods, are earnestness, wild sanctimony, and faux transparency. For he was not in the business of the shapeless blurt. His business was the making of art, and to trace the pattern of his autobiographical verse . . . is to watch a man breaking and remaking the mold in which the soft mass of his experience—his adventures in sensation and dread, as well as his erudition—may be poured. It would be gross to claim that he warped and wounded his life, and the lives of others, in order to nurture his poetry. He was a genuine victim of psychological vastation, not a fraud. Equally, though, he found nothing in his life which he could not use, or reuse, within a line of verse; his troubles were *trouvailles.* (86)

The lamenting Lane is not the only critic fearful that the confessional poetic ideal has been bastardized by common use. Yet, in all the discussions about the surge of personal narratives across diverse marketing niches—and there are many such conversations happening—the term not being invoked, at least not in any positive sense, is "composition." This is understandable, given our disciplinary history—our connection of freshman essays with "shapeless blurts"—but such disassociation is nonetheless strange. Composition as a concept and as a field has the potential to make the "personal turn" in the academy (the *return* to the personal aesthetic in composition studies) yield prose distinctive for its aesthetic appeal, its logical soundness, and its investigative proficiency, for its intimate qualities, its critical acumen, and its social work.

We can start the recovery of this term by drawing on one of our oldest disciplinary practices: definition. "Composition," by definition, *Webster's Revised Unabridged Dictionary* informs us, is the "art of composing . . . by placing together and uniting different things." It works through "synthesis as opposed to analysis." The second edition of the *Oxford English Dictionary* is not so restrictive. It lists twenty-six different historical meanings, including three central to composition studies. Composition is "an intellectual production," "a train of ideas put into words," and, significantly, "the combination of personal qualities that make any one what he is." Although its definition is briefer and more compact, *Webster's*, too, attempts something of a history, listing the term's familiar domains in the arts, the language classroom, and the courts, which is to say, in the discipline we have come to call "composition and rhetoric." Composition is ours for the keeping if we find the term valuable enough to hold on to.

Is this yet another academic game of "what's in a name"? Wouldn't "essay" or "creative nonfiction" or "literary nonfiction" suit just as well? Genres, like metaphors, define, which is to say that they open and close possibilities by delineating.[1] Put simply, composition as a term, as a concept, as a genre, can do work that other genres cannot, which does not make these other genres inferior, but simply different.

Academic Writing: The Case for and Against

The frequently maligned academic article does important intellectual work, distinct from commercial and literary writing. I, for one, am not ready to dispense with the academic enterprise. But critics do have a point: Academic articles are frequently dense and difficult, too cold and distant in stance and voice for a good number of readers, including the general public and the students whom such pieces are presumed to benefit. By their very studied nature, these articles are not timely. Academic articles are thorny enough that they even come under criticism from other academicians. Consider, for example, Peter Elbow (2000), making his strongest case for academic discourse: "I love what's in academic discourse: learning, intelligence, sophistication—even mere facts and naked summaries of articles and books; I love reasoning, inference and evidence; I love theory. But I hate academic discourse" (235). Elbow continues by describing academic discourse as "author-evacuated prose," a phrase he borrows from Clifford Geertz. Such a critique seems to make sense and has been persuasive to many. It seems to suggest a land of milk and honey, a way to talk about things academic in a different way, in a beautiful and moving way. Still, one need only substitute terms in Elbow's argument to see the claim's restrictions: "I love what's in poetry: the sublime evocation of experience—even compact images and inverted syntax; I love the rhythm, the rhymes, the evocations; I love the compressed lyric. But I hate poetry." Elbow would argue that my substitution accords "special honor to *form*" and holds true mostly for poetry in its "ideal" form (60). It ignores, he would continue, the kind of prose that can be paraphrased. To which I would respond, Yes, paraphrase—and its cousin, translation—are possible and valuable strategies. They are, however, different—structurally, semantically, and contextually—from the originals that generate them. Something has been changed, or as we usually say, something has been lost.[2] Finally, however, Elbow softens his stance on academic discourse, explaining that he is attempting to construct not so much an argument against academic discourse, but rather one for a "*kind* of nonacademic discourse that is particularly important to teach . . . discourse that tries to render experience rather than explain it" (237). And on this point he is joined by others.

The Personal Essay: The Case Against

Essays, particularly personal essays, have a long, rich, and deep relationship to composition history. I love the form, I have practiced it, I will continue to practice it. The essays that form the middle section of this book are meaningful to me and moving, I hope, to at least some readers. But, as critics argue, personal experience narratives have serious limitations. They argue a "case of one" under the vexed claim of "universal truth," and they are frequently known, as the Lane critique (2003) reminds us, to play on emotion, sensation, and trauma. They are often predicated on the idea of a single, buried, unified, "authentic" voice that the writer must uncover, rather than on the idea of an array of socialized voices that writers compose out of. They may work to close rather than open intellectual dialogue, to prompt, as Gesa Kirsch (2001) explains, this response: "How can we respond without denying the personal? How can we be critical without dismissing personal experiences?" (57).[3] Others share Anthony Lane's (2003) conviction that "confessional" narratives are, or should be, about art rather than expression.[4] To the degree that such narratives are literary, a quality some (but not all) writing instructors insist on, they become what Lopate (1995, 2001) labels "personal essays," a form that functions at its elusive best by making a reader think and feel and appreciate all in the same moment. Finally, the aim of essays found in small literary magazines is aesthetic, perhaps at the expense of the critical, the political, and the emotional. The point is worth underscoring: If the personal experience narrative central to many late-twentieth-century composition classes thrived on emotion, then its professional equivalent, the belletristic essay, like academic writing, deplored "sentiment," especially if it's "personal."[5]

The twin poles of academic and personal writing formed the core of many a late-twentieth-century composition debate.[6] More recent forays into service learning have led the field in the direction of public argument and civic engagement. To a certain extent, the recent interest in creative nonfiction, with its roots in journalism, can be read as a movement toward this new civic engagement, an interest in the timely, the immediate. (It can also be read, accurately, as a yearning for the good old days of personal experience narratives or for the gentlemanly days of belles lettres.[7]) To see the civic connection, we must focus our attention on creative nonfiction's ties to literary journalism, its attempts to deliver "human interest" news by using the techniques of poetry and fiction. Literary journalism does entail means and ends that would be of value to composition classrooms. Investigative reports and moving declarations can singe a reader's consciousness, change deeply held beliefs, perhaps even move one to action, to change, in the civic arena. But, again, we can easily discern the form's drawbacks: Such reports and declarations rely on facts chosen in great part for interest and currency and emotional appeal, and are rarely compromised by an academic complexity that readers might find tedious.

Here in the twenty-first century we sit, as Elbow (1990) so aptly puts it, in our "almost universal commonplace that what is personal and expressive must be at war with what is social or public" (13). And sit we will continue to do, rehashing old arguments, if we continue to vacillate between standard genres that make us choose, to use one of Elbow's (2000) phrases again, between "being an academic" and "being a writer" (379). Composition, by its very composite nature, can undo these generic ties and reassemble them into a form that achieves all these disparate aims. It is perhaps why we are drawn to it. And drawn to it we are, again and again in our professional debates.

The Search for Form: Composition in the Late Twentieth and Early 21st Centuries

"Process" has been perhaps the most influential concept in late-twentieth-century composition scholarship and practice. Who of the initiated new generation of composition instructors doesn't teach through drafting and revision long after Flower and Hayes's protocols have faded in the discipline's collective memory? Despite this shift to process, the last four decades are most marked by changes in its antithesis: product. The years have seen a series of critical camps enlarging our concept of what writing instruction should comprise. While the focus has been on first-year composition's purposes—to introduce students to the academy; to help them to understand their own lives, to express their own voices, to do the civic work of fighting injustice or enacting citizenship—the most concrete results have been the shifts in the kinds of products students compose, most of which are recognizable only as classroom genres. A glance at the last few decades of textbooks reveals the shift from personal experience and research papers, to academic discourse, to forms of formal argument, to public fieldwork, and now, if interest holds, to creative nonfiction.

One way of viewing this shifting landscape, the glass-half-empty view, focuses on market demands. Textbook companies, in order to be profitable, need to issue new or revised books. Shifts in pedagogy result not just in different student products, but also in new, marketable professional products—and their imitators. So goes one refrain. Yet, just as often as the textbook lament, we hear another cause for these shifts, that they are symptomatic of composition's systemic identity crisis. We change so much because it is fashionable to do research borrowing from other fields. The barrage of critical positions has been, to put it mildly, jarring to many. Here, for example, is Kurt Spellmeyer's (1996) wonderfully cranky response to yet another "paradigm shift" in composition studies: "It would be pleasant to think that professors of English, concerned as they are with both language and style, might be able to see through the ruse of fashion, but no: for us, in fact, fashion is nearly everything. As our profession's first century comes to a close, what do we really have to show for it all, other than a sad parade of styles, beginning with philology and ending, for today, with the movement known as 'cultural studies'?" (425).

Somehow, declaring oneself to be an unfashionable, fussy teacher of composition still marks one's academic caste, stresses what we do (process again?) rather than what we produce and teach—a recognizable written product, distinct from that produced by our colleagues in literary studies and creative writing. Although we have as a whole embraced process, we have continued as a field to do battle over product, and seemingly will continue to do so. Whatever product we light on, I argue, we need to avoid hugging the monologic extremes that have polarized the field, though even these extremes have been productive in determining the generic possibilities and limits of composition. If scholars such as Peter Elbow and Patricia Bizzell have polarized the field, they have also galvanized and energized it, deepened its intellectual premises. And, as their appearance on the same Conference on College Composition and Communication panel in 2001 suggests, they're moving closer rather than further apart. Bizzell (1999, 2000) is engaging the personal with her idea of "hybrid academic discourse";[8] Elbow (2000) is showing an increased appreciation for academic writing. As a field, it seems, we're ready to discover, to borrow Kurt Spellmeyer's (1993) image, some common ground. Even though I write personal essays, it makes me nervous to hear and read the chants against academic writing, the backlash to personal writing, the simplistic renderings of *Personal is better and closer to the writer* and *Academic is better and more socially responsible.* It likewise makes me nervous to imagine composition as creative writing's misfit stepchild. We've covered and re-covered that ground. Collectively, we know the promise and the pitfalls of the purely academic, the purely personal, and the purely aesthetic.[9]

Still, one can begin with these same premises and discover the half-full glass: What all our varied approaches to first-year composition solidify is that some form of nonfiction is the customary genre for composition classes, the thing inside and outside the university for which we are known. Robert Atwan (1995) uses the narrower term "essay" to make the point: "No matter what theoretical basis a composition program subscribes to—whether it's oriented to the writing process, collaborative writing, critical thinking, etc.—the goal is always the same: the production of essays" (23). If one accepts that nonfiction—not belletristic essays, but rather compositions—has been the province of college writing and will continue to be, then these questions follow:

1. What kinds of nonfiction should we be writing?
2. What value is this product? (i.e., how can we judge its quality? its aesthetic value? its academic worth? its pedagogical worth?)
3. How can we articulate, describe, and teach to our students this kind of product?

These questions do not necessarily throw us back into the quaint, long tradition of essay writing—despite some efforts to return to this belletristic territory—but instead, if we choose, directly into postmodern debates.[10]

As I sit down to compose, I ponder, how might I make an academic piece expressive? an expressive piece academic? And, most difficult of all for me as an academically trained writer, a narrative theorist, and an essayist, how might I now use techniques of investigative journalism to extend my inquiry still further? These are challenges I welcome, even when I fail. This, for me, is the luxury of being in composition studies at the start of the twenty-first century: We don't have to choose between forms of nonfiction, ways of knowing, unless we as a field continue to deny our roots in composition. Composition as a form has the potential to fuse the personal, either first- or third-person, with the academic; to bridge the gap between our identities as teachers and scholars; to provide the remedy for feeling, to borrow Harriet Malinowitz's (2003) words, "split, dissatisfied, frustrated, compromised, and resigned" (310). In order for this to work, however, we need to know more, formally, about the possibilities and the range of this hybrid form. We have to overcome the problems of "too few models for those attempting such a hybrid genre, little if any encouragement to risk it, and no guidelines for how to do it well" (312). We have to start authoring and transforming the publishing venues available to us. Once we do this, we may find that we have a subject—composition—as well as a process to teach. Composition can become ours, is in fact already ours by definition, if we are bold enough to claim it.

Notes

1. I'm borrowing here from George Lakoff and Mark Johnson's influential *Metaphors We Live By* (1980). The problem of definition, however, is one that scholars of the essay frequently confront. See, for instance, Carl H. Klaus (1995) distinguishing between "montage," "collage," and "disjunctive" to define the structure of a particular type of essay: "They're all approximations of a sort, metaphors for a kind of essay that's far too complex to grasp in a single word. Still, some of these metaphors, some of these terms, are not just more accurate than others. Some are more suggestive and illuminating than others" (44).

2. Elbow's stance on academic writing is actually more complex than is represented by this example. In several of the essays collected in *Everyone Can Write* (2000), he returns to the issue. While at times he suggests that he chooses to be a "writer" rather than an "academic," the form of the essays he has written (largely academic, but interspersed with richly voiced personal narratives) shows that Elbow practices what he hopes his students might learn: He wants his "students to feel themselves as writers and feel themselves as academics" (379). His main point is that we're missing something when we exclude the personal, and here Elbow and I are on the same page.

3. Ellen Cushman (2001) reads something a bit unseemly in the "consumption" of personal narratives: "I strongly disagree," she writes, "with the ways in which self-disclosures like [Victor Villanueva's in *Bootstraps*] are consumed and commodified by readers. Readers' values drive up demand for

more self-disclosure if the story is sensational, or suppress self-disclosures if the story is not a hot commodity" (57).

4. For further reflections on the confessional (and a rare defense of the form), see Melissa Goldthwaite's "Confessionals" (2003).

5. "A review that calls a work 'sentimental' is understood as a damaging judgment. The author's rationality is in question, and so is the credibility of the argument" (Clark 1994, 101). For a history and a critique of the anti-sentimental modern criticism, see Clark's persuasive work, *Sentimental Modernism* (1991). Religious faith, still linked perhaps with the tradition of nineteenth-century women's sentimental writing, suffers the same critical response: "Current norms for personal narratives written by academics militate against religion," explains Anne Gere (2001, 47). "'Don't discuss religion,' my mother admonished me, 'if you want to keep your friends.' She did not mention keeping my job, but I learned early in my career that it was better to keep some things to myself, especially religion" (46).

6. Spellmeyer's *Common Ground* (1993) and Elbow's *Everyone Can Write* (2003) provide excellent overviews.

7. See, for example, Cynthia Selfe's "To His Nibs, G. Douglas Atkins—Just in Case You're Serious about Your Not-So-Modest Proposal" (2000) and Atkins's (2000) response.

8. See also Bruce McComiskey's (2002) discussion of the "new integrationist movement" (751) and, in particular, "social expressivist discourse" (752) in his review of Robert Yagelski's *Literacy Matters.* Paul Kameen's review essay, "Re-covering Self in Composition" (1999), covers similar territory. Barbara Kamler's *Relocating the Personal: A Critical Writing Pedagogy* (2001), Cristina Kirklighter's *Traversing the Democratic Borders of the Essay* (2002), and *Alt Dis: Alternative Discourse and the Academy* (Schroeder, Fox, and Bizzell 2002) provide other, very different models and arguments for integrative work.

9. For a summary of critiques of personal/process writing and for his critique of academic discourse, especially in relation to the essay, see chapter 4 of Spellmeyer's *Common Ground* (1993). The debate continues: See Doug Hesse's "The Recent Rise of Literary Nonfiction: A Cautionary Assay" (1991), Min-Zhan Lu and Bruce Horner's "The Problematic of Experience: Redefining Critical Work in Ethnography and Pedagogy" (1998), Susan Miller's "Comment on 'A Common Ground: The Essay in Academe'" (1990), and Susan Welsch's "Writing: In and With the World" (1995). Elbow (2000) also provides in-depth, point-by-point summaries of the debates.

10. Doug Hesse (1991) best articulates the problems of adopting classic and modern literary forms for use in postmodern classrooms: "The politics of canon formation is old these days, but we in composition studies must understand that its issues pertain to us, too" (326). Such an insight forces us to understand that "the essay as natural . . . cannot exist," is not "purely independent of other texts" (328).

Part I

Children at All Costs

Female Quixotes

Sometime in 1997, I was in midconversation with a colleague—another professor in the English department, another woman—when I realized I was late for my annual checkup. I remember the conversation mostly because it was one of those that float easily across professional and personal boundaries. By a circuitous route, we had ended up talking about Tabitha Gilman Tenney's 1801 *Female Quixotism*, an early U.S. novel modeled after the classic *Don Quixote*. In her midthirties, the heroine of Tenney's novel is ancient history—she has to carefully pick the "white hairs" from her "jetty lock" (1801, 111). She is almost as foolish as that other figure invoked by early novelists, the female pedant. It was the reference to aging that jolted me into remembering my annual checkup. I was almost forty.

We live in a time when female passion throughout life is not only accepted but expected. Unlike women two hundred years ago, my professional colleagues, most in their late thirties or forties, talk candidly and freely in academic corridors about womanly matters—romance, postmodern criticism, feminism, philosophy, sex, the best bedtime stories. Yes, sexism still exists in the academy, but times are better for women, and we know it. We fit in our world.

But, later that particular day, I found myself ever so slightly bothered in my comfortable world, in part because I was no longer in it. I had walked to the university health clinic complex, where the HMO office is inconveniently located in a completely different building from the women's health clinic, which is housed in the place where real disease resides, the hospital, whose closest neighbor is the cancer center. I arrived just a little late to the upholstered cubicle, where I gave my name and numbers in response to the receptionist's prompts. Her third question threw me.

"Are you pregnant?"

She asked the question directly, without even blinking. *Such a personal question*, I thought, noticing for the first time the pictures of smiling children taped to and around her computer, distinguishing her cubby from the other three identical ones. "No," I answered, realizing, on second thought, that it was a fair question. She needed to know where to send me, and in the world of women's health, everything depends on where one sits on that slippery slope between fertility and menopause. She sent me on my way, and I walked to the hospital building, hoping I could get this annual ritual over quickly and get back to the place where I frame and pose the questions.

Once in the women's health clinic, I was not scolded for being tardy, so I settled in. I was neither nervous nor apprehensive. Over the ten years I'd been a patient at the clinic, I'd come to know the routine well. I'd seen several doctors—not because I'm a difficult patient, but because this is a teaching and research facility. Generalists come to retrain in infertility or high-risk pregnancy and then move on to positions elsewhere. I'd been to one doctor I really liked, but I no longer qualified for him. He was on the high-risk pregnancy side of the center, the side where I'd seen the unforgettable sonograms of blighted ova—things that once pulsed in me, dead on the screen.

But I wasn't focusing on those sonograms that day. It's cliché, but those days are gone: We have two beautiful children, sons adopted at ages two and a half and three from a Russian orphanage. I'm thankful to be on the other side, the hopelessly infertile and menopausal side, even though I and most of my friends are in some unnamed medical category in between.

I'd chosen a new doctor and expected to like her. We were close in age. I had worked with her when she was reviewing surgical options with a Russian refugee. I wasn't there as a Russian–English translator. That had been tried, but it hadn't worked, because the refugee had left the office believing she had cancer rather than severe dysplasia, or carcinoma in situ, often referred to as "pre-cancer" cells. I was there because the Russian woman understood my English; I knew to speak slowly and e-nun-ci-ate, to continually rephrase and repeat the ideas I was trying to convey, to put the stress on the wrong part of the word so that pre-CANCER (as if cancer needs any highlighting) becomes PRE-cancer. I was there to translate medical English into understandable English.

Despite her med-speak, the doctor impressed me. I liked how much time she spent with her patient—as much time as her patient needed to make the best choice—and how persuasively she argued for the more aggressive surgical loop excision, or LEEP, option. I was also impressed that she heard, really heard, when the refugee woman laid out a problem all too common. Her husband, who had studied and worked as an engineer in the Soviet Union, now had a job mixing chemicals, a job with few virtues except a health insurance plan. But the insurance was only covering 75 percent, and they were responsible for the other 25 percent. While she wanted the LEEP surgery to better her chance of eliminating the risk of a cancer her grandmother had died from and her mother was battling, they just couldn't afford their 25 percent. They had to go with the cheaper cryotherapy option, which had a high rate of failing to deter the progression of cervical cancer.

The doctor left the room to negotiate with billing up front. The negotiations failed, so she did something bolder. She waived the difference by putting a different code in the chart. She would do the more aggressive LEEP surgery and record the less expensive cryotherapy. It was illegal, to be sure, but I thought it heroic, the stuff of a novel or a film: Young, attractive (a must for Hollywood) female physician battles impersonal medical institution. The script appealed to me. A female Thoreau moving to the beat of her own pulsing conscience. It made my heart beat a little faster.

When I met this doctor again, this time as a patient, she brought with her my very thick chart. I knew that she hadn't had time to read it and that she would ask me the usual questions, the answers to which are in the file. It's life in a university health clinic, where we enjoy good care despite such inconveniences. I'm used to med-speak, and I was prepared to answer everything, so we were making good time, rolling through the questions, until we hit the complication: "Do you have any children?"

I did hesitate, but only for a second; two, tops. "Yes," I said, watching as she wrote; "two boys." I could see her form the number 2. "We've adopted two boys."

She paused without looking up and crossed out what she had written. "So you have no children." It was a statement, not a question.

"No, no children," I said, a female Judas, knowing that, professional or not, my days were scheduled around park visits and preschool and meals and snacks and bedtime stories, knowing that the sun rises and sets, the moon rises and illuminates, by the light of those two boys, my children, my sons.

But behind the gold bank vault doors of the university women's clinic, I stuck to the only code she (so excellent a listener) would hear me say. *No children.* I imagined other women, their stories rewritten in shorthand, codified into pages of charts that become part of medical research, lined up, color coded, organized, and managed.

The rest of the exam went quickly, and I was soon ready for checkout. But the receptionist was on the phone. She shrugged at me to indicate that her phone conversation had gone on too long already; someone was putting a cog in their machine. "When was your appointment?" the receptionist asked into the phone, presumably not for the first time. She was wearing a white polyester uniform with a pattern of cheerful teddy bears. She repeated the question, somewhat more abruptly this time, trying to reel the speaker in, to finish with the one on the line so she could move on to me. And then I thought I must be hearing wrong, because nobody could be so brutal. "Where did you *have* your miscarriage? Was it here?" she interrogated. "Which doctor?" After a short moment with the receiver, she looked satisfied. She'd made her catch, and with a few more efficient words, she hung it up.

She turned to me, glancing at the checkout slip on the top of my chart. "Oh," she said. "You don't need a follow-up. You didn't have to wait."

I couldn't believe it when I heard myself thank her, when I added, "No problem." No problem?

For a second I wanted to turn and fight, to battle them—or better yet, I thought, infiltrate and break their code. But I knew I wouldn't.

Even could I invent some new words, they would not accomplish heroic feats. Inside the center for women's health, behind their gold doors, I am not woman enough. I am merely quixotic, my words as comic a weapon as a sword against windmills.

Peter Pan

> Peter Pan *is sometimes scoffed at for the excessive and cloying nature of its innocence. It is in fact one of the most fragmented and troubled works in the history of children's fiction.*
>
> —Jacqueline Rose, *The Case of Peter Pan*

I

When he was five years old, my older son was enamored of Peter Pan. We owned at least three versions of the book, which we read again and again, even though the story always turned out the same. Sometimes we didn't read, we just reenacted. My son would pick up a stick. "It's a sword," he'd crow. "I'm Peter Pan, you're Wendy. Let's fly!"

"Do you know the way?" I'd ask awkwardly. He wanted me to play, but I was new to child's play. I gloss texts for my profession and pleasure—I'm not used to texts glossing me. But my son hadn't such worries. In 1997, two years after his adoption, he was five. He was then, as he is now, slight, with a muscular frame, blond hair, gray-green eyes, and light, smooth skin too perfect even for the sun to burn. He is a dancer, all motion and energy and imagination. He played happily with sticks that doubled as swords, hangers that doubled as hooks. The way to Never Land was clear to him.

"Second star to the right, and straight on till morning. Here. Here's your fairy dust. We're off. Oh no, there's Hook! Where's my sword? Aha! It's here! Take that, Hook. Ticktock, ticktock, ticktock. I got him. Yes!"

And so we played for some years. Daddy was always Hook, I, the ever-aging Wendy. It was appropriate, for, like Wendy, I flew to Never Land, or at least a place that seems as far—the Arkhangelsk province of Russia—to bring children back to our Darling household.

Why Russia? In the early 1990s, adoption in this country was narrated as a Pan-like adventure, complete with the ticking of Hook's biological crocodile clock. Men flew into bedrooms asserting their paternal rights. I wanted simple plots and naively thought I could find them, evade the complex and downright ugly by flying to another country. And so fly I did, in search of simplicity, above forests and rivers and oceans, to Moscow, to a sea captain's flat in Arkhangelsk, to adventure. And, having taken such a journey once, I am compelled, like Wendy, to age and repeat it.

II

Peter Pan, I find, is a classic, a familiar story. It is also, I have discovered, one that people suspect. What would motivate someone to care for—to love—someone else's children, cold children from a cold land we were still basically at cold war with?

Peter Pan, if you believe the critics, is not such an innocent tale. J. M. Barrie created the story to entertain a young boy he befriended in a park. At the death of the boy's mother, who had become a friend of Barrie's as well, the author assumed guardianship for the boy and his siblings. The arrangements were strange by our standards: The children continued to live in the house they had shared with their mother; Barrie stayed in an apartment close by.

Odd enough. But the literary story turns again. In his 1902 novel *The Little White Bird*, Barrie writes the relationship between the boy and man as sinister. The narrator, it seems, has invented the story of *Peter Pan* out of twisted intention: to capture the imagination of a boy he plans to steal. As critic Jacqueline Rose (1984) notes, biographers narrate J. M. Barrie's life as the "story of a man and five small boys, whom he picked up, stole and possessed" (2). In these Freudian accounts of J. M. Barrie's art and life, "an adult's desire for a child" becomes necessarily sexual. Parenting becomes pedophilia, adoption suspect. A person who adopts children, especially a single man (or divorced one), is guilty, a wide net of association cast around the actions of a felonious few. Yet even married couples cannot escape modern skepticism. When we are willing to grant in our cultural narratives purity of motives to adoptive parents, we feel comfortable only if we note defects in the children, those damaged goods that saintly folks will care for, or if we assign villainy to the parents who "abandoned" the child. Villains, formally speaking, are not entitled to a point of view, are not allowed sympathetic interior monologue, and are not allowed to voice understandable motives, to justify or explain their parts in the drama.

I want it to be about love. I want Jacqueline Rose to forget Freud long enough to see that *Peter Pan* in all its versions is a troubling, fragmented, beautiful story about a troubling, fragmented, beautiful act: adoption. I want her to see adoption as a classic, complex, familiar, and, yes, innocent story.

III

Never Land is a far-off place. It takes time to get there. One must fly through blank spaces and wade through pages of print. It took me five years and many, many words.

But, on a Saturday in January 1995, all goes better than planned. I am finally at the gate waiting for the flight to Moscow; I am using the time to study Russian. A Russian-speaking woman arrives suddenly, holding a rather large baby in one arm and her lower back in the other hand. She is escorted by an airport employee who knows absolutely no Russian.

"Can anyone here speak both Russian and English?" he asks in a voice that evinces doubt that anyone could be so bilingual.

And then the fun begins. A woman translates for us all. The woman carrying the rather large baby has hurt her back. Another woman who is waiting is a masseuse. Can it be arranged? Why, of course! As Russians are fond of saying, "In Russia, anything is possible!" They clear some chairs and set up a massage parlor: The woman with the hurt back enjoys a full, vigorous back massage; the translator has her neck worked on. Because I have attempted to say a few words in Russian, I am chosen third and receive as my prize a full back massage in O'Hare International Airport. When I step onto the plane, I have friends, and they are Russian.

What could possibly go wrong in a country where anything is possible?

IV

In lands of possibility, much can go wrong. In 1992, the year my son Alexej was born, much did go wrong in newly democratic Russia, the place he was born.

I am trying to imagine my son Alexej's birth. It is the cold Russian winter of 1992, and food is not circulating. But each time I try to imagine it—here from the comfortable vantage of America—Truth and Ignorance trip me up like cartoon bullies. What little I know comes from documents and from an interview with the orphanage director. I don't know and can't ever verify the truths surrounding my sons' adoptions. I am working off documents like this one:

> The boy was received from city hospital accompanied by medical nurse. Fifth pregnancy child. The mother was observed in the prenatal care dispensary for rheumatism, mitral valve incompetence, circulation insufficiency I, complicated with a toxemia of pregnancy. The mother's timely labor was complicated with the secondary weakness of birth activity and prolonged stage of pushing, treated with oxytocin stimulation.
>
> As the manifestations of intranatal trauma, cephalohematoma and 10 × 14 cm back hematoma were noted. After hemostatic therapy, packed red cells transfusion and the hematomas were cured.
>
> The child was taken from children's hospital by his mother's arbitrary decision. Further treatment was not administered because of mother's refusal.
>
> Postnatal diagnosis: the perinatal damage of the central nervous system, mainly spinal cord; intranatal trauma of the thoracic part of the vertebral column; mild spastic paraparesis of lower extremities; cephalohematoma, hematoma of the back; acute asthmatic bronchitis.

From what I gather from Russians close to the process—Russians bound by agreement to protect the privacy of all parties involved—the health certificate exaggerated Alyosha's health problems so that he would have a better chance of being adopted by foreign citizens. But, even without this rumor, I've learned to suspect all documents. Alyosha has three birth certificates, each listing a different place of birth or different parents. (On one certificate, we are listed as the parents and Moscow as the place of birth.) The facts are slippery. But then I have little else, despite my meager investigating efforts while in the orphanage director's office. It was investigative journalism gone wrong, maybe because I was just too interested to ask the right questions.

The director's office was small, a bit crowded, but neatly arranged. The large conference table was surrounded by scratched file cabinets and the director's old wooden desk. In this setting, I was surprised most by the thick Persian rugs on the walls and under the table; that is, until the doctor in her crisp, white medical coat pulled out blue and gold Russian china and set an elegant table: small porcelain plates; teacups and saucers; an array of cakes, preserves, and chocolates; and a samovar. Over tea and chocolates, we discussed Alexej's short three-year past.

"Where is his mother?" I asked.

The orphanage director shrugged. "He doesn't know," the translator said. "She's not from here; she's not known."

"And her other son?" I had read that Alyosha had a brother, Petja, five years older.

Another shrug.

"Will she know about the adoption?"

"No," the translator said quickly before anyone answered, obviously trying to assure me that I wouldn't be traced and found. No one seemed to understand that I was digging for information. The translator continued, "She will know only that he's been adopted, that she no longer must pay the fine, that's all. No names, no addresses." He showed me again a document I'd seen before.

> Parents: Father is entered on the birth certificate according to mother's words. Mother—Irena Nikolaevna Petrova[1] is a single mother—evades bringing up her son. She was deprived of her parental rights according to the judgment of the District People's Court.
>
> During the boy's stay in the orphanage none of the relatives were interested in the child's life, called him by telephone, visited him, or wrote letters.

> Child was suggested for adoption to Russian citizens but there were no persons wishing to adopt him.
>
> Administration of the city orphanage gives its consent to the adoption of this child by foreign citizens.

She's unfit; she's lost all her rights to this child. They all but said it.

"Will she at least know he's in another country?"

The nuance of "at least" was lost. "No," he replied again, obviously trying to assure me that bureaucratic inefficiencies in two countries, as well as time and distance, unpredictable economic fluctuations, and different languages, would make tracking us impossible.

I was enjoying their hospitality—tea, cakes, chocolates, children. In Russia, adoption is secretive. I could not, without making a chasm between us, convey that I wished for her to know that he would be in America, that I wished her to have pictures and news, if she wished, to watch him grow through print and photos.

"Spaseeba," I said quietly, "thank you," and took my tea, Russian-style, with jam. It was, after all, why I was there in Never Land to begin with. It was, after all, I who changed in the course of the journey.

V

Tea, it seems, is a temporary thing. Even in the director's closed, congenial office, Irena Nikolaevna Petrova hovered outside the barred window, an unspoken voice that was heard nonetheless.

It is the cold Russian winter of 1992, the year my son Alexej is born. Food is not circulating. I am thirty-eight years old and pregnant again, for the fifth time. My lover is at sea, where he will stay several months. I have a heart condition and rheumatism, so this, like my other pregnancies, is a difficult one for me. This is my fifth time, but I have only one child, a boy, six years old.

I travel from the village to the nearby town to have my baby. I know nobody who lives there, but there is a dispensary and a hospital. My babies, I have learned, need them to survive.

The birth, like the pregnancy, is difficult. I push for a long time, but to no avail. Finally, labor is induced and I give birth to a live infant, a boy, Alexej, whom they immediately take from me and transfuse. They wish to keep him—he needs further treatment, they say—but I can't afford such treatment. I take him home with me.

But the winter makes it impossible. I can't get food; I can't keep him warm. He is sick and small, and he breathes with difficulty, rasping. After six months, he stops growing. I know I must leave him in their care, and I know that if I do so, I will not see him again. I cannot pay the money exacted by the courts. Perhaps in the future?

But no, our future is so uncertain. I turn him over to a nurse. After losing children through miscarriages and stillbirth, I lose a six-month-old son. He will not remember that I said good-bye.

As we sign the adoption papers, it is impossible for me not to imagine that I hear Alyosha's mother speak a story like this one, a story outside the presumptions of the printed versions, outside the presumptions about women "who give up their children." When I look at Alyosha, I don't want to see a haggard woman showing more than her years, hacking on nicotine, glassy eyed from vodka, leaning on bars, seducing sailors. If she knows her son has been adopted, I hope she thinks well of me, rejecting the stereotypes of ugly Americans staying in their three-hundred-dollar-a-night hotels, complaining of all things broken and dirty, looking only for imports, never venturing into old government stores, anxious at the airport to leave only with their souvenir *malchik* dolls and as few memories as possible. I want her to know that I sang him to sleep in Russian, in a Russian hotel; that I ate schi and borscht, cod liver and kasha; that I shopped on the streets and in the government stores that lingered despite the new capitalism.

Alyosha's mother and I: We've too much between us to think ill of one another, and too little to know the truth. We might as well think well of one another.

VI

At one point, I wanted to own my children outright, like other people, with as many guarantees as possible. Adoption seemed such a risky venture, particularly when the principal was shared, as it is in open adoptions. I went to Russia so I didn't have to share, not realizing the irony of traveling to a newly capitalistic country to make a safe investment.

And, in some ways, it worked. I know little about my children's parents. *Be careful what you wish for*, goes the old adage. I wanted boys who would fit right in; I wanted difference invisible to the eye. We gave them American names: William and Richard. But we don't use those. Instead, I find myself pronouncing their Russian names, finding delight in the new ways my tongue and mouth move—Alexej, Alyosha, Aleksandr, Sanya. We share our children with the Russian refugees and immigrants we meet. "Our children were born in Russia," I mark their difference, acknowledging the land of their birth, their origins, with pride. But with that pride comes a strong desire to know more about those origins. *Be careful what you wish for.*

"Such clever boys," "Such handsome boys," the Russians say when we encounter them at the playground. It is bitter cold out, and in such weather, the playground is mostly empty. Still, we are there, and the Russians are there, Jewish families mostly, escaping to central Kentucky from burning synagogues or threats much more vague but no less dangerous. "Come by our house," "Meet us at the park tomorrow," they invite us. In their sparsely furnished two-bedroom apartment with white walls and beige furniture, the deep red Turkish rug hangs foreign above the old TV set and the secondhand VCR. Our new friends marvel at Alyosha's and Sanya's alien registration cards, their green cards—at how quickly the documents arrived for us. They offer the boys jam with hot water for a treat, recite Russian verses, sing Russian songs, and both cheer and lament as my sons become American and monolingual, as their mother tongue refuses to roll in the familiar ways, as the Russian language they barely remember takes on my American accent.

Or we meet a colleague who works at our university. He has recently been to Moscow after several years' absence. "The gold domes, did you see them? They are back; beautiful. You might not have noticed because you didn't see what was there before. But they're back; beautiful." He pauses. "But there are other things you cannot possibly know because you weren't there before. The social services have collapsed . . ."

"Yes," I remind him. "That's why we have our children." We nod our heads, both perhaps hearing the silence differently, but convinced, for now, that we share a perspective. *They are Russian boys.* They link us—strangers—with the truly foreign: the safety of communism, the risk of capitalism with no safety nets.

VII

"I am not happy with you," I say, breaking once again the cardinal 1990s rule of child care: Don't confuse the behavior with the child. Alyosha has gotten in trouble for what seems the hundredth time in one day, some sort of personal best record for bad behavior. My patience has first worn thin and then given out completely. "Alyosha, I am just not happy with you!"

In just a little over a year, he's forgotten Russian almost entirely and learned English well. His gray eyes brighten green, a sharp glower. "Well, I'm very angry with you too. I'm going to Russia, to live with my Russia mommy. And you're going to be very sad."

I feel my maternity slipping away and know I must have it back. It would be so easy at times like these to strike down his mother, cast her out with words, but I know the move is fatal, that we—Alyosha and I—need her. "Alyosha, we don't know where your Russian mommy is. She couldn't take care of you. And yes, I would be sad without you. Before you came, I was very sad because I needed a child and didn't have one. And you needed a mama because yours couldn't take care of you."

Miraculously, he picks up the thread—it's a story we've told before, and it turns out that whatever has possessed him has left at least this part of him his usual best self. And with his usual best self return the smile and the words we're accustomed to hearing.

"Yes, and I was crying, 'I need a mommy.' And then you came and we came to America. I'm American now and you're my mommy."

"Right. You're Russian American," I correct him and continue. "I saw you sitting on the floor, playing with a Woodstock bird. You looked up and you were smiling, and I knew we would love each other."

And I did know it. The rug of the playroom I remember distinctly because it was not a beautiful Persian rug like I'd seen elsewhere in the most humble of places, but instead some strange Russian rendition of indoor-outdoor carpeting. The toys were stacked neatly in glass-topped cabinets that extended the entire length of one wall. The toys themselves stacked: pyramids formed of rings, each successively smaller; nesting *matrioshka* dolls with nearly identical hollow women fitting one into the other, enveloping the small, solid doll at the heart of the toy. The orphanage officials had dressed Alyosha in thick tights typical for both boys and girls in Russia. His were red. And on his feet they had placed, no doubt for my appreciation, big Disney cartoon slippers, made stranger by the fact that they were the wrong mouse, Minnie instead of Mickey. Later, after taking Alyosha to the toilet, they returned him dressed in a pale pink, striped short set, complete with pink tights and the Minnie Mouse slippers.

But all these details came later. What I remember clearly and immediately are his smile—his smile!—and the word he spoke with enthusiasm as soon as I entered the room: "Mama!" He was one month shy of three years old, old enough to understand, and he had been waiting for me. I was all nerves walking into that playroom, coming into motherhood, but he settled me, took all the strangeness away with his smile that comes not from his lips and teeth, but from his eyes, gray eyes, pale eyes that brighten green, more powerful, more effective than words or touch. This kid was magic.

It is that magic that I miss when gray glowers green. I know those moments must come and will go, but I feel, at those moments, bereft of motherhood and self. When his bright self returns, as it has today, I feel confident and solid again. "Suppose," Freudian critic Jacqueline Rose (1984) writes, "that what is at stake in *Peter Pan* is the adult's desire for the child" (3). Suppose.

"I knew we would love each other," I repeat.

"Yes," Alyosha continues, his best self speaking, his gray eyes working, "and my Russia mommy and daddy are dead."

Dead. It's not the first time I've heard him say it, so I'm prepared to rescue them again, bring them back to life—or at least I think I am. "We don't know that, Alyosha. We don't know where they are. They just couldn't feed you, or keep you warm enough, or buy you medicine. You were sick . . ."

I let my voice trail off, congratulating myself on the coolness, the age-appropriateness of my answer. But, as with all self-congratulation, this comes too soon.

"Yes, I know they're dead. My Russia mommy and daddy are dead. They talk to me from heaven sometimes."

It's not the heaven part that throws me but the talking, the communication. I let him have the last word because it's a fantasy I understand. If I do the right thing, if I listen very carefully, I can hear them myself.

VIII

Not all our times are so contentious or heavy. Most of the time with Alyosha, I fly high in fantasy. We are constantly telling each other stories; often we are the heroes. Lately we have been planning an elaborate trip to Russia.

But there are limits, of course, to fantasy, and our second son, Sanya, seems placed as the realist among us. Alyosha's health records predicted a very sick child; we received one in perfect health. Alyosha napped on schedule and slept soundly through the night. From the beginning, he let me hold him, read to him, and sing him to sleep. His only malady was delayed speech, which he instantly set about correcting, clearing developmental delays and learning a new language so that after a year's time he tested above average American children in syntax and vocabulary. At his worst, Alyosha is a green glower; at his second worst, he is a born con artist, working his mark with a charm that overcomes his least subtle attempts: We know we are being worked and succumb cheerfully.

While Alyosha's body was and is small and strong, Sanya's when he arrived in October of 1996 was big-boned and, well, a little fat. Sanya's health was predicted to be good—and has been, if you discount what was called level-two rickets and inactive TB (both of which have been successfully treated). For several hours after Sanya arrived by train in Arkhangelsk, he would not let me hold him, or even touch him. He relented when I gave him suckers or raisins, fed to him one by one. For the first two months, he spent most of his time sitting and eating. His very large blue eyes, intensified by his pale skin and light brown hair, surprisingly expressed very little. He did not sleep through most nights, nor did he nap. His favorite word was "morning," which translated to him as "awake." He was, and sometimes still is, an odd combination of insecurity and will. Sanya, too, came with speech delays, an affliction that he reminded us of several times a day. At least for the first two months we knew him, he showed little compulsion to learn language. He knew the dozen or so survival words, including "morning," but past those, he resorted to a high-pitched, through-your-skin scream (at six years old he became, no surprise, an opera buff). It was amazingly effective, fantastic, but it was not the stuff that fantasies are made of.

In fact, from beginning to end, Sanya's adoption was different. Alyosha's adoption was four months long, from the time we filed with the Immigration and Naturalization Service (the first official step in the process) until the time I traveled to Russia to bring him back. Sanya's adoption took only a month longer. Yet Alyosha's adoption process felt interminably long, Sanya's painfully fast.

I thought of little else during Alyosha's adoption. Although I was teaching at the university, and probably pursuing my research, it was the adoption that was at the front of my mind. I began each day with phone calls, checking with the various agencies to see what documents needed to be signed, which needed a notary, which an apostille. I drove to the state capital and hand carried documents for signatures. Because I couldn't contact the INS or the FBI directly (they were processing our fingerprints and doing criminal background checks), I hounded our senator's office. I did the feathering-the-nest stuff with wallpaper and paint and bought the kind of children's furniture that can only be called cute.

All was going well, quickly; it seemed as if we might have a child by Christmas 1994, although we hadn't yet received INS approval. And then came the obstacle, the one I couldn't drive my way through or over. The Russian Duma met and recommended that international adoptions be halted until the laws were changed. Yeltsin was expected to sign. All adoptions would be suspended for at least six months (such suspensions are common occurrences in international adoption, no matter the country). Christmas was bleak. But the new year opened with promise. The ever-surprising Boris Yeltsin actually sent the recommendation back to the Duma for clarification. Our senator pressed the INS for approval, we received permission to proceed, and by the third week in January of 1995, I was on that plane to Russia.

From the beginning, I knew I wanted more than one child, particularly if we adopted. I thought there would be some solace in having a sibling adopted from the same place in the world. The tie that binds would be geography rather than blood. I wanted to get both boys in one trip (efficiency), but my husband objected. "Let's try it," he said cautiously, "and see how it works. Then maybe we can try again, you know, naturally." After Alyosha's adoption, we decided not to "try": adoption was certain, pregnancy wasn't. But before we could submit the paperwork, trouble struck.

The problem with Sanya's adoption was my mother, which takes some explaining. My mother was thrilled about our adopting, and three months or so after Alyosha came home, as soon as she could arrange a two-week stretch of time off from her work at a Catholic church, she flew from California to Kentucky for a visit and lavished all the attention a Hallmark grandmother heaps on a grandchild. All was well, except that we noticed during the visit that she was slurring words—perplexing, as she wasn't a drinker. By the time she flew home after two weeks, she was also dragging one foot. By the next spring, her speech was so slurred that we began corresponding almost exclusively through e-mail. What followed for the next six months was a series of diagnoses and misdiagnoses, until the disease progressed to a clear etiology: amyotrophic lateral sclerosis, ALS, or Lou Gehrig's disease.

Sanya's adoption now constantly struggled for center stage. My mother was anxious that the adoption go through; she wanted to meet and know him. But I felt, irrationally, that if I could delay the progress on the adoption, I could delay the progress of her disease, which was rapidly advancing. In the spring of 1996, partly at her urging, we filed the INS papers that began Sanya's adoption.

Shortly after the papers were filed, Alyosha and I made a trip to California, and I saw my mother for the first time since speech had left her. Alyosha and I came, of course, bearing gifts. We bought her a CD player and some CDs. I chose something light and whimsical: MGM musical hits. She listened to the first track, something like Jimmy Durante's "As Time Goes By," moved her head as if dancing, and then began crying, all the time still dancing with her upper body. She tried to move to the next track but, thankfully, did not yet know where the right buttons were and hit Stop. We took the chance to give her the music that Alyosha, then four years old, had chosen: the soundtrack from one of his favorite movies, *The Secret of Roan Inish*, a film about a lost child, and a seal that transforms herself into a woman, a wife, a mother, but all the time longs to be free of her body. Eventually, she is freed as she gives into her longing, shedding her human skin and slipping back into the sea. My mother listened to the music intently, thoughtfully. Her hands formed a T.

"That means 'thank you,'" my sisters told us.

My mother put on her headphones and the *Roan Inish* soundtrack to drown out noise and distractions while she ate her lunch. And, though I couldn't hear the music, I distinctly saw two images: the woman from the film, looking out to sea, longing to shed her human skin; and my mother, concentrating on bringing the blended food from bowl to lips, collecting the extra with napkins, clearing with faint noises the minute grains that, despite their pureed smoothness, deposited in the folds of her throat.

After a few weeks, I returned to Kentucky to teach summer school, but my thoughts were continually in California. My mother e-mailed me, giving me an account of her health, but mostly asking about the adoption in progress. When she learned that our papers had been processed and that we had a referral, a two-year-old boy, she called.

"California Relay Operator No. 221. Please hold one second while I connect you to your party."

I heard her sound, the one I had learned over the past months, a keyboard clicking. I pictured her on the other end with a headset, typing intently. I waited until the sound stopped to hear the stranger translate, "It's Mom. What's happening with the adoption? Go ahead."

I explained I was traveling in September. "Go ahead," I said.

"Come soon. Go ahead," the mother/operator said.

"Yes, of course. We'll come Christmas. Go ahead."

"Perfect. And your party has hung up."

In late October, I traveled to Russia to bring home Sanya. It was nothing like the first time. Sanya was malnourished. He had needs, he was needy, he needed all of me and more. I was emotionally spent before I even bought the ticket.

By Thanksgiving, my sister, the one who can put a sunny face on any situation, was calling to tell me I needed to bring Sanya to California *immediately.* My mother wouldn't die until she met him and was rescinding her hospice orders not to be resuscitated. Hospice was threatening to pull out. We had to come if her dying was to be done right.

"Let me finish the semester," I said. "I'll be out Christmas." I knew before I even finished what she would say. I boarded a plane with Sanya a few days later.

"There's something soulful about him," my mother scrawled on her pad. "He gets right in my heart." She moved her hand to her chest, striking it gently, like an old-time Catholic during the consecration of the Host. *This kid is starved for love.* She didn't need words to say it; I knew what she meant. There were moments when he looked at me just the way that woman in *Roan Inish* looked off to sea, knowing he belonged but wondering how to make the journey. I wasn't the proverbial beacon in the storm; I wasn't even strong enough to send up flares, to show him where to find me, but he kept trying. After his initial resistance, Sanya loved to be held, insisted on it. His legs, bowed from malnutrition, curved themselves naturally around my waist. But as an orphan child, he was unaccustomed to this thing for which his malnourished body was so perfectly suited. He never knew quite where to put his head (such an intimate decision): on my shoulder left or right, on my breast. Once, in those first weeks, when he let me hold him, his legs slid easily into place while his head tensed and then began the usual rocking and rolling, rolling and pitching, pitching and pulling, from side to side, down and back, until finally it completely missed any maternal mark and blacked my eye. There we were, shipwrecked again.

My mother died about a week after Sanya and I arrived. Alyosha and my husband flew to California for the funeral. After the funeral, my husband rushed back for finals. I and the two kids returned together a week or so later. I had missed the last weeks of the semester and final exams, and I had student evaluations to face. I was tired of planes and travel, but mostly angry that the whole thing had ended. While Alyosha slept, I sat up, tense, listening to Sanya scream "morning" the whole flight back.

It took me time and grieving, but I finally discovered that I did have a love story to tell about Sanya, though different from my love-at-first-sight meeting with Alyosha in the orphanage playroom. My mother was right: He has a powerful, almost unmatched capacity to love and be loved. He naturally reaches for a person's hand or puts an arm around a shoulder. He leaves all of us love notes around the house. Best of all, I like to picture him as a small child, sitting relaxed in his red wagon, or as a six-year-old at his first opera, his light brown hair wispy across half-closed eyes, lips slightly parted, with a look of ecstasy and contentment—the look of being at sea, at home.

IX

"When we go to Russia," I tell Alyosha, "we'll start in Moscow, visiting friends. Then we'll head to St. Petersburg, and perhaps stay there for a month or so during the summer. We can make a trip to Arkhangelsk to see the orphanage."

Alyosha interrupts, as he often does, to add a detail or raise a question. This time, it's a stunner, concerning, of course, Sanya. "Can we see Sanya's mother?"

Sanya's mother. Technically, we could arrange a meeting with Sanya's mother. She has always been easy for officials to find, was always available to sign documents. Because of changing adoption laws, she was compelled, over a period of two and a half years, to relinquish her rights to her son three different times: first by refusing to answer official letters, second by signing her name to a letter prepared for her, and third by writing the letter in her own hand. She was sixteen when she gave birth, almost nineteen by the time the law completely recognized that she seriously and finally relinquished her son. We have never told either boy this. But we also never told them that we didn't know where she was. Alyosha made a simple deduction, completed our act of omission.

It's an omission I pay for: How does one explain to a young child that a young mother, now a little older, might not want to be found? In *Peter Pan*, Barrie (1906) is brutal on the subject:

> [Peter] went in a great hurry . . . because he had dreamt that his mother was crying, and he knew what was the great thing she cried for, and that a hug from her splendid Peter would quickly make her to smile. Oh! He felt sure of it, and so eager was he to be nestling in her arms that this time he flew straight to the window, which was always to be open for him.
>
> But the window was closed, and there were iron bars on it, and peering inside he saw his mother sleeping peacefully with her arm around another little boy.
>
> Peter called, "Mother! Mother!" but she heard him not; in vain he beat his little limbs against the iron bars. He had to fly back, sobbing, to the Gardens, and he never saw his dear again. What a glorious boy he had meant to be to her! Ah, Peter! we who have made the great mistake, how differently we should all act at the second chance. But Solomon was right—there is no second chance, not for most of us. When we reach the window it is Lock-out Time. The iron bars are up for life. (40)

If Alyosha prompts visions of Peter Pan's fantastic flights, Sanya reminds me that Peter Pan was a boy who suffered. To tell of my romance with Sanya, I have to employ realism, all the more brutal in its impact because I have to confront the real consequences of flight and fancy. I have to be able to see that, with only a change in time and place, Sanya's mother's story, like Alyosha's mother's, could have been my own. And I have to acknowledge that I like the story of Alyosha's mother better.

X

"You have been pregnant four times and you have no children?" the doctor asks me with genuine Gradgrindian consternation. *How could science have failed us?* In 1994, I learned that I am what the medical profession calls a "habitual aborter," someone who experiences repeated, unexplained, spontaneous miscarriages in the first trimester, the kind usually attributed to Darwinian natural selection, some abnormality in the fetuses. But Darwin didn't work in my case. When the fetal tissue was picked out of the blood, pickled in solution, and tested, it was found normal. I, it seems, was the one not naturally selected for reproduction.

"Yes," I say. "Four times. No children. That's why I'm here for the physical. We're adopting." The doctor knows what I know, that only three of the four abortions were spontaneous. He doesn't, of course, know the details: that the first pink science-kit dot emerged unambiguously just three weeks after I learned that the man I had called my own was married to someone else, that he had effectively disappeared, that the pink dot was as unreal and flimsy an image as the man himself. Yes, like Alyosha's mother, I have had repeated, tragic, unfruitful pregnancies. And, like Sanya's mother, I have been young, unmarried, unwanted, and pregnant. I understand Lock-out Time. "Affliction," one feminist theologian writes, "can be having what you do not want or wanting what you do not have." I understood both kinds of affliction that day in the doctor's office when I held nothing in my arms. Before I left the exam room, the doctor promised to get the letters written quickly. In what seems to me one of the very few real acts of contrition I've ever witnessed, he did.

XI

From Russia, I bring home a souvenir, a *malchik* doll. The boy stands eighteen inches high and has blond hair, a pale plastic face, and blue eyes. The irony of this souvenir is not lost on the Soviet people who produce and sell it. Adoption in Russia (and America, and Central America, and China) is big business. And, like any big business, it's easily imagined as a sordid, greedy operation. While Russian officials thank us for helping with their "orphan problem," Soviet people bemoan the loss of national treasures and cite the trend as another negative Western capitalistic influence: inflation, drugs, street gangs, AIDS, international baby selling.

To Russia, I thought: *Less involved. No visible difference.* It had been awhile since I'd seen an *Adventures of Rocky and Bullwinkle* cartoon or, for that matter, *The New Adventures of Johnny Quest,* where all the Russians speak with bad accents and worse intentions. No, differences aren't erased by whiteness: History comes along for the ride whether we like it or not. Only my ignorant conflation of discrimination with racism, two completely separable terms and experiences, led me to believe I'd found the simple route. Now I discovered that, in adopting abroad rather than domestically, we'd managed to avoid the Mexican and Civil Wars, but had stepped right into the cold war.

I've given up on simplicity now, I'm listening now, so I weigh the sides. What would my sons' lives have been like had we not dirtied our hands? Thankfully, in this sense, Russia does seem to make the question a little less complicated. Any major social change would have come too late for my sons, especially for Sanya, whose rickety bones were set to calcify into malnourished deformity at any moment, whose lungs seemed poised to blossom into full tubercular bloom. The Soviet system had already collapsed, and with it, my sons' homes and their prospects. They were forced into either state homes or market ones. Would our sons have been better sitting on the orphanage shelf like so many clean, unpurchased *malchik* dolls? Isn't it, after all, a biblical promise? "I will not leave you orphans; I will come to you" (John 14:18).

As for the "best interests of the child" arguments, I skip fairly rapidly over those. Children adjust—that's what's so frightening, and real, about Barrie's Lost Boys. It's adults who struggle (witness the Baby Jessica case). I'll never agree that birth parents are always best, yet I'll never figure out the measure for when children should go elsewhere; I'll never agree that people living in poverty don't have the right to have children—lots of them, if they wish—and I'll never convince myself that money has nothing to do with a child's livelihood and future.

Yes, with some ease, I can stack the rhetorical deck in our favor until I hear what Soviet people say; indeed, what Americans against transracial adoptions say: "If parents had the resources to keep their children, if we made the lives of these children materially better in their own homes . . ."

So the question hangs out there: Is it too late for Russian children of the future? It is a land of complex voices. I hear that voice—*our future is so uncertain*—the voice of students I visited at the Arkhangelsk Pedagogical Institute, the voice of Alyosha's mother. But I hear also the voice of the woman at the airport and feel the strong fingers pressing deeply into the muscle tissue of my back—*in Russia, anything is possible.*

XII

A good many people, I have learned, say what's on their minds. And so, when I hear the question that grates on adoptive parents' nerves, the "How much did your children cost?" question, I am prepared with an answer, graciously provided by my family: my niece Nicole is the Cadillac kid in our family.

She was born all but dead. "Like a deflated ball," my brother said over the phone. Her major organs—liver, kidneys, lungs—all had shut down. "They ran IVs through her," he continued, "and she plumped and pinked right up. But they couldn't get her blood to clot. It was all water."

It had been, by all measures, a difficult birth. Nicole had to be transferred to the special children's hospital two hours away; her mother couldn't be moved. My brother stayed with his wife, and when the hospital moved the baby out, they held each other and, I think for the first time in their married life, grieved together. They were not ready to say good-bye. Circumstances being what they were, they did. Nicole's first pictures are of a baby splayed like a frog on a dissection table, attached to tubes attached to machines, covered with a glass dome.

After it was clear that she would live, we all worried about the cost of such advanced life-saving technology, or rather, about how my brother would pay for it. Would their insurance cover it all: the special ambulance, the special machines, the special facility? How would two young people manage, with a mortgage and a fledgling business? Would they lose everything? Eventually, their story ended happily. They were reunited with their baby at the children's hospital; their business survived. All is well. Had circumstances been different, had Nicole's health records decided whether she lived in an institution or a home, she would have been one of the unadoptable, the unwanted, overfilling the overseas orphanages or our own foster homes. I am tempted to say that, in this country, such issues resolve themselves. But would Nicole be alive had she been born to folks who arrived at the emergency room without a medical insurance card? Would such medical magic have been performed had she been born to braceros, legal citizens or illegal workers who pick the crops in the nearby Salinas valley? Nicole was one expensive child, the MVP of our family, easily topping my other niece's difficult birth and our two adoptions combined. "The Million-Dollar Baby," we joke. Yet few would accuse her parents of buying their child, of paying money for her. Few would complain that the hospital charged for an extra box of tissues or an extra pint of blood; few would find the fees for attending physicians outrageous—not even those who would accuse Russian officials, who live in circumstances much less grand than most American physicians, of profiting from children. Adoption is somehow different. *Where does all that money go?*

There is one simple truth I've learned through this whole alternate, well-traveled path to motherhood, and this is it: All children cost. We are willing to pay exorbitant prices for them—to have them at any cost. And for good reason: They are worth it.

XIII

It seems everyone in America has opinions about abortion, about morning-after pills, about children giving birth to and raising children, about welfare mothers. When speculation arose that the Clintons might adopt (in pre-Monica days), political commentators considered the angles: The president and first lady couldn't adopt a small white baby, as that would be too elitist or racist or even criminal ("buying a baby"); they couldn't adopt an older child in foster care (potentially incurable psychological problems); nor could they adopt an African American or mixed child, for fear of alienating some minority group; they certainly couldn't adopt internationally, as that might cast aspersions on the American foster care system; nor could they adopt a Native American child, as that would raise issues of tribal sovereignty. If I remember correctly, it was decided that a Latino baby would be just the right political choice.

We're not the Clintons, so I've been surprised at how many people not only have opinions, but are compelled to share them with us. Some people romanticize what we've done: "Those children are so fortunate." Others are suspicious: "Why do you want someone else's children? You didn't take them from their parents, I hope." Still others are scientifically obsessed: "Do you know the medical histories of their parents?"—as if generations of Americans, not to mention people around the globe, cannot live full lives without the wonders of genetic tracking; as if children, like some dogs, come with pedigrees; as if children, like some cars, come with warranties. A few continue to see Red: "Why Russia?" Our children, it seems, cause people anxiety about the future: We might not know what we've got.

Like Wendy, I flew to a far-off place and returned with orphan children. As with all parenting, it has been an adventure, uncertain by definition. Still, there are things I want to know. I want to know my sons' parents, but not to vilify them for breaking cords, not to learn their gene pool and health history. Like many people interested in tracking down kin, I want to know them because they are part of my family. Like many people who receive anonymous gifts, I want to track down the donor. Like many people estranged from those they love, I want to know that they're OK, that their lives are full and satisfying by some measure, not necessarily mine. As it is, I have more than they (a stable career, for example, in a country where a stable career is somewhat possible). And now, I have something that was theirs. Something very valuable.

XIV

Peter Pan ends in fantasy, with the Lost Boys adopted by the Darling family. Each night, the Lost Boys hear bedtime stories, the fictional magic that lured Pan from Never Land, tempted him to give up boyhood for family. For us, too, such fantasies are crucial. We tell the story of our family's birth, substituting words for photo albums filled with smiling, precious infants. Our children were not photographed until they became valuable. Their first photographs advertise their health, show all their limbs and what they are capable of doing—running, walking, eating, dressing, using the pot. They were simple photographs, yet we used them as the occasion demanded, turning them into medical records, passing them to expert physicians for inspection.

Only in fiction can we make amends for such treachery, can we rescue a different sense of value, of worth, of children spoiled and pampered by things like bikes and Legos—things that, under capitalism, spell love. This also J. M. Barrie (1911) understood, and so his Pan brought to the Lost Boys a mother, to read them fictions: "And then at last they all got into bed for Wendy's story, the story they loved best. . . . 'Listen, then,' said Wendy, settling down to her story" (163–64).

But ours isn't the Disney version; it's life, and we need to hear the voices left behind, to be reminded of the larger, classic, more complex tale. Occasionally, our stories get updated. Against the advice of other Americans who have adopted internationally, we have sporadically asked for more information. "You don't want to know," they tell us. Several years ago, we heard that Alyosha's older brother, Petja, had been located. "He is in boarding school," our facilitator wrote, not understanding that the privileged connotation of "boarding school" made the phrase an impossible translation choice. "If they answer our letter, I'll send the translation."

"They have found Petja," I told my husband when I got the news.

"Is this good news?" he asked.

"Yes," I replied, "it is."

"What do we do now?"

"Good question. Get a bigger house?"

"Impossible."

He was right, and I knew it. As a ten-year-old, Petja would never be adopted, for any number of reasons—would not even be put up for adoption. His future is grim. One Internet source claims that, according to a 1995 report by Russia's Ministry of Education, "one-third of all Russian orphans will commit suicide before the end of life. One-half of the boys will join the Mafia, and one-half of the girls will become prostitutes" (Hope International 2000). Chilling predictions, perhaps sensationalized. Perhaps not.

No translated letter ever arrived. We will probably never know more than Petja's name and birth date. We will likely never see a photograph.

XV

Back home in Kentucky, throughout most of the warm southern year, we leave the windows open. We worry neither about chills nor about those who hover outside our windows, Pan-like, unchanging, listening to our stories: lost mothers and fathers, fixed in time—an unwed teen, a tragic thirty-eight-year-old who has lost her children—members of our family, leading quiet Russian lives in a country where the future is uncertain and the past is filled with loss.

My name is Irena Nikolaevna Petrova
  My son Alyosha fell from the pram
  He is one of the Lost Boys
  I don't know where he is.
My name is Marina Ivanovna Aleva
  My son Sanya fell from the pram
  He is one of the Lost Boys
  I don't know where he is.

My name is Pavlova Olga Maximovna
  My son Vasha fell from the pram
  He is one of the Lost Boys
  I don't know where he is.

Barrie's *Peter Pan* is a wartime classic. It's sinister only in that it's a common, tragic story, repeatable any time parties go to war, no matter how frigid the landscape, no matter how cold the war. It's the very stuff of children's literature, of children's lives. At least it's the stuff of our lives.

Note

1. Her name, of course, has been changed.

Houses I

Life Without Children, or Spring Cleaning 1994

Some lovers live together without children and are happy. We were not. Or rather, I was not. My husband finds contentment living in the present. For me, longing is a pleasurable state, especially if fulfillment follows quickly on its heels. I longed for children.

When I met my future husband, in 1989, I was living with my cat and a chocolate Lab in a small, nineteenth-century shotgun house located between the university where I worked and a struggling downtown. He lived alone in a two-thousand-square-foot new house in a gated community near the interstate. I was renting with an option to buy. He owned his house. When we decided to throw our lots together, it made sense that I and my pets should move in with him.

We lived in his house for five years without children, and every childless spring, I wanted a divorce. It was an unsettling springtime ritual, as predictable as a Memorial Day sale. For university professors, spring marks the near end of the long academic year, the buildup of exams and papers and research and correspondence. We are flat-out tired in the spring.

Summer is entirely different. At the end of summer, we are rested. The ends of those childless summers were no exception. Each summer, I was in love again and convinced that my brusque New Yorker husband was the most compatible mate imaginable. A perfect fit, we were and are.

But T. S. Eliot was right: April is the cruelest month. And those springs spent in my husband's house were particularly trying. Not because of flowers blooming and warm weather prompting the young to shed their clothes and roll unprivately on lawns—these were all mild distractions, enough to provoke a smile, an erotic thought or two, but not a divorce.

No, there's something else about spring, something that convinces me we've had it wrong all these years. Spring isn't about romance, except in the lightest, newest sense, the Paris-spring-runway sense. What spring is really about is streamlining, unburdening, casting off. It's about making things uncluttered and clear. It's about getting rid of anything even the tiniest bit complicated. In a word, it's about spring *cleaning*, which leaves me as bare as a raked spring garden, full of promise, but finally empty.

I know about spring cleaning. My mother cleaned obsessively as soon as the days began to lengthen significantly. It was some kind of residual Yankee ritual, even though, by the time I was a teen, she had lived most of her life in New England's geographic antithesis: California. She kept the spring motions even when the tasks were illusory. We had no winter wardrobes to put up, no attics to move seasonal clothes to.

She wasn't a good housekeeper, generally. She was a person who lived three seasons in less than orderly surroundings—our ironing board was a constant fixture in our kitchen, stacked with clothes, some folded, some not. But, come spring, her closets would meticulously organize, the summer colors—all the fabrics were the same—would magically gravitate to the center, the grout on her bathroom tiles would whiten, and her kitchen would become neatly assembled, just shy of labeled.

I inherited much of my mother's temperament, including her proclivity for clutter. But mine is unrestrained by any New England upbringing. I am California born and this, together with the academic calendar, probably explains why my spring cleaning urges get recognized at best only once every other summer. It's not that I'm without pattern or ritual: For the first few months in a new apartment or house, my rooms are always enviably neat, every book, vase, painting, or photograph placed for effect. Inevitably, by midterm, the living spaces have degenerated into "homely"; by finals, everything, including dust, is covered by files or books or papers; every flat surface becomes a cluttered desk. Neither husband nor children nor an aging live-in in-law (he joined us the month we adopted Alyosha) has changed my pattern. I live on a regular basis with a high tolerance for chaos and clutter.

My husband, on the other hand, has a strange relationship to clutter. He's a mathematician, and his office is littered with old offprints, tax records, financial papers, and stacked boxes of files from a *Bleak House*–like lawsuit that ran in the background of his life for almost twenty years (he'd done some calculations for an aborted sale of a Kentucky coal company). He is stereotypically absentminded. But his home in the gated community was a different matter, maybe because it was a postdivorce house. In this new space, he preferred a focused Shaker aesthetic, or perhaps the ideal theorem—the trim, simple, elegant solution to historically complex problems. He loved the feel and look of cherry and ash, deplored artificial varnishes, and forbade furniture polish, the ultimate bourgeois vulgarity. His furniture was not dusted once a week, but instead occasionally stroked and revitalized with various combinations of warm mineral and linseed oils. The wood was unadorned: Even a vase or a picture frame was junk to him. He liked walls without color. He didn't believe a house needed to be painted—ever—unless its inhabitants were particularly dirty. So, when I complained about the white walls in his house, particularly after we took on another dog (a surprisingly effective consolation for another miscarriage), he began a harangue about the dogs and me and how we were all just too dirty to live anywhere nice.

"Paint," I replied. "People paint walls. All the time. Sometimes just for a change. They put color on them, patterns."

He was not persuaded. We scrubbed—or rather, he scrubbed, as I had proven myself neither acceptably schooled nor skilled in the art. By the time we moved, he'd cleaned the walls so often that the flat paint was just a shiny discoloration, oily rather than dingy, like bad skin.

Still, in the first few years, when we were childless, the house was not such a bad fit. I was untenured and supposed to be concentrating on research, not yard work or neighbors. We traveled with some frequency, leaving our lawn to be fertilized and mowed along with the golf course greens. It was not a house I would have chosen, but before his white walls became shiny, people used to say my husband had a nice house, and he did, I suppose, though it was surely limited in the kind of life it could offer us. Its main feature was light—windows in every room that looked west to a setting sun, reflecting off water. Beautiful enough. But it didn't stand up under scrutiny. Located in Kentucky, it could have been anywhere. The water, after all, was an artificial pond, part of an overly manicured golf course, and the golf course was bounded by a road quickly becoming a highway of loud freight trucks, belching out their testimony to a thriving market economy. The house's location at the edge of town and its gated security made it a place cut off.

It was usually in the spring, after a winter indoors with the walls, after two semesters of teaching, after too much accumulation, that the perfect fit of our marriage became a little too tight. In what can only be described as a snit, my usually spacey mathematician stalked the flat surfaces of our house, eradicating clutter, throwing baby and bathwater to the fates. Because we were both academics, papers were sacred, but everything else he flung into the dumpster. One time he threw away a perfectly beautiful family snapshot: in it his father is sitting in an adirondack chair, holding his baby son. It was clearly not taken as art, but there it was, beautifully aligned, exquisitely shadowed, like finding an old silver dollar in a button collection. It was my fault, it turned out, that the photo had to be pitched. I picked up an old frame for a dollar at a garage sale. (I thought it was maple, but—heavens!—come to discover, it was sealed with varnish.) I wanted just the right picture, so in the frame I placed the one I'd always admired in the drawer, the black and white photograph of my husband cradled in his father's lap, the laundry blowing in the background.

So, my first offense: I put the photo in that frame. But it wasn't just the frame that was offensive. It was where I put it. I placed it in the room with the prized oval cherry table, surrounded by chairs with spindles of ash and cherry forming high, wide arches, soft to the touch, sensual in their curves. I put it next to this set, on the matching cherry glove table.

It was several days before I noticed the photograph missing, several days after his last spring-cleaning fit, and I'd yet to discover all the possessions that had met their ends.

"Where's the photograph of you and your father?" I asked.

"I threw it away." No apologies in his tone; indeed, vindication.

"You threw it away?" I repeated, thinking, *Surely he just tossed the frame. The photograph he must have saved.* "You kept the photo, right?"

It was his usual spring response: "I don't have time to separate garbage."

That it was a family picture didn't matter. It was his family, after all, so he had rights.

Eventually, his spring-cleaning jag ended, at least for then, for that time. But the whole thing was as predictable as spring itself, just as disturbing as T. S. Eliot's famous lilacs forcing themselves out of the dark, dead land. What more might my mathematician, in the throes of anti-sentimentalism, toss? What might I, living in such proximity, be moved to pitch?

Divorce, I thought. *It's certain. It's spring.*

But then the lazy Kentucky summer came, and we weathered—indeed, even enjoyed—the climate of another year. And so it went, spring after spring, until we found our children and at last, three years later, moved into an older, Depression-era home, into a house that was ours and embraced us, clutter and all.

Part II

Love at All Costs

Consider what else was lost, along with the sentimental.
—Suzanne Clark, *Sentimental Modernism*

Modern Fidelity

A few years back, my husband stopped reading my essays. Actually, that's not entirely true. He never really started reading them with great enthusiasm. I just talked him into reading three—probably exactly the number of his theoretical math publications in the field of operator theory that he talked me into slogging through. Of course, I had him read the essay about our children. "What happened to me?" he said. "It's all about you."

"Well, yes, of course. It's a personal essay. It's just the genre. But if you want me to write you in . . ."

It took no time at all for him to refuse the offer. "I think I'm better off out of it. Your pieces are all too sad."

He'd only read one other piece at that point—one about my mother dying. When I told him I'd written again about my mother, he said, "Uh huh," while he watched the stock numbers race across the TV screen. When I pressed him about it, he said, still watching the numbers, "The stuff about your mother just makes me cry." He knew my mother.

"Not this piece," I said. But he didn't believe me. It seemed he wasn't going to risk being waylaid by sentiment—either that or the pages were starting to add up, and reading was starting to be work.

Finally, though, I think it was sentiment that made him so resistant, which put me in an odd position. As an academic trained in the late twentieth century, I had been taught to deplore sentiment with the kind of scorn reserved for Reader's Digest Condensed Versions. Yet when I tried to write about my mother in a modern, ironic voice, it just rang false, like a uniform that identified me with a club I didn't want to belong to. I found myself more and more in sympathy with some nineteenth-century sentimental women writers, women like Almira Hart Lincoln Phelps, whose voice changed after her daughter's death in a train accident, or women who lost husbands and children on the violent slave auction blocks or in one of the bloodiest wars this country has ever experienced. How could ironic distance possibly suffice in such historical instances? T. S. Eliot managed it, but he was a banker, used to the abstraction of numbers.

In the aftermath of September 11, we rediscovered sentiment, irony's antithesis, and one hopes that we are exploring it in all its complexities. Sentiment done badly, overdone, is difficult to defend. But is there room for women writing sentiment, doing it well, after the turn of the twenty-first century? (There's long been room for male sentiment in the changing literary canon.) Can female sentiment ever be considered art?

I

> *In Tomorrow one voice does for all. But it is a little unsure of itself; it keeps testing itself.*
>
> —E. B. White, "The World of Tomorrow" (1939)

Not the least fascinating part of the *New Yorker* is the obsessive interest it breeds in its own history. Some former staffer, it seems, is always reminiscing about the magazine's golden days, promising to reveal some secret about its inner workings or, more frequently, some piece of gossip about its high-profile editors and writers. Although I live now, and have always lived, in places decidedly removed from New York City, I confess that I am one of those who eagerly await the newest offering from the *New Yorker* memoir industry.

For scholarly purposes, of course. It's difficult to conceive of the essay's place in the literature of the twentieth-century United States without recognizing the magazine's profound influence. And the more I read, the more I'm convinced that the essay as we know it owes much to the love affair that started between E. B. White and Katharine Sergeant Angell[1] sometime in the late 1920s. Katharine, who joined Harold Ross's editorial team almost at the *New Yorker*'s inception, met E. B., or "Andy," White when she extended an invitation to him to change his status from freelance contributor to permanent staff writer. Eventually, their workplace relationship grew into a love affair, and, as with most great western romances, it began as an adulterous one. In the summer of 1928, Katharine Sergeant Angell traveled with her first husband to France, where, as she had planned, she consummated her first and only adulterous affair. After the time in France, Katharine returned to her husband briefly, but tiring of *his* repeated, indiscreet infidelities, she left him. Because her husband refused to grant her the customary full custody of her children, she also effectively left them. Shortly after her divorce in 1929, she married the younger Andy White, and thereafter denied that their affair had ever occurred.

Both Katharine and Andy were thoroughly modern, though in different ways. His preoccupation was, as he described in a 1936 letter to his wife, with machines that "are against man, and are simply lying in wait for all of us" (1976, 138). Although the theme of encroaching technology influences most of his best work, including his often-reprinted "Once More to the Lake" which he wrote during his five-year interlude at *Harper's*), it is perhaps most visible in his disconcerting review of the 1939 World's Fair, in which he doubts and resists a technology-driven view of the future and, Robert Frost–like, laments the loss of rural pleasures. It's hard to imagine what a resurrected Andy White would think of the fully technologized U.S. society that has moved into the next millennium. Horror comes to mind. But my guess is that White and other crusty U.S. moderns would feel almost fresh again, with all the scary millennial talk of disintegrating family values, scientific disasters, and other impending terrors. The technology of the new millennium—warp speed, compact volumes—carries the worry of its Achilles' code, its alarming default set to loose a chaotic flow of information or make it disappear entirely with one trip of a binary. How much data can we fit on the head of a pin? And what do we do with it all? How much noisy data can we filter out when precise surveillance is what we need? Presumably, information technology will beget an instability unknown to previous generations, a new millennial postmodernism. Postmodernism squared, if you will. But, despite all the talk and media hype, modernism is still very much with us. If E. B. White predicted accurately one facet of the future, it is this: Tomorrow's voice does indeed seem singular and unsure, testing itself over and over again. Perhaps nothing revealed this better than the late-1990s increased interest in memoir—and the literati's simultaneous disdain for and dismissal of the form as part of some new sentimentalism.

Although no less emblematic, Katharine's modern ideas differed from her second husband's. She demanded fidelity in a partner and wedded herself to an engrossing career. She was willing to sacrifice full control of her children's care to secure such fidelity. This trend—women forsaking their traditional roles, entering the workplace—worried her Victorian father, who urged her to stay with her husband, to keep the appearance of marriage, because, as he put it, he hated to see her "dear children become victims to these modern ideas of individuality" (Davis 1989, 80) He needn't have worried. All three of Katharine's children grew into prosperous adults. Her son from her first marriage, Roger Angell, is a long-time fiction editor (and writer) for the *New Yorker*. Her marriage to Andy was long and happy, enduring until her death forty-seven years later. At the end of her life, Katharine was a sight: aged, bloated, covered with sores. Yet, by all accounts, Andy seemed only to see the beautiful and imposing young editor he met, wooed, and wed, the Bryn Mawr graduate who covered their bed in manuscripts.

Katharine would never become as well known as her writer-husband. He survives as one of the essayists most anthologized. His reworking of William Strunk's Cornell textbook, *The Elements of Style*, is routinely recommended for writers, both beginning and professional, and frequently makes one or another "best books" list. Yet those who reflect (and reflect again) on the legacy of the *New Yorker* often timidly posit that Katharine was perhaps as influential. Though she began and ended her career as a writer of magazine essays, she made her deep marks through her less visible work as an editor of fiction, memoir, and casual essays at the *New Yorker*. For at least thirty-five years, first under the legendary editor Harold Ross and later under the equally legendary Willliam Shawn, Katharine edited and influenced.

Together, then, the Whites helped shape the voice of Tomorrow; together, they made voice in the U.S. essay tradition a family affair.

II

> *Episodes of love . . . appear in the modern, rational conversation, the discourse of our times, as something to be gotten over, grown out of.*
>
> —Suzanne Clark, *Sentimental Modernism*

It was just a little more than three decades ago, close to a half-century after Katharine and Andy shook things up with their affair, that "modern ideas" spread into our small town in California's rural San Joaquin Valley. That famous *New Yorker* cover, the one where most of the United States becomes a suburb of New York City, had suddenly become not simply funny, a classic instance of ironic overstatement, but prophetic. Even as an oblivious teenager, I could feel the change advancing like the overblown menace in some sci-fi horror flick. The town banded and resisted: Eyes became more vigilant, ears listened for the slightest indiscreet whispers, relatives worked with even more energy to patch up marriages or hurry them up.

It was during this time, in the mid-1970s, that I found myself part of a family watched. It was through no indiscretion of ours: My father died suddenly and young, leaving a young wife of forty-two and four children ranging in age from nine to seventeen. No longer traditionally nuclear, we became the real thing—unstable, potentially reactive. We attempted a kind of microlevel détente, doing the best we could to maintain appearances, to fashion ourselves the picture of stability. My mother stayed away from the desperate restlessness of singles groups located in larger neighboring cities. She continued to attach herself awkwardly to the couples with whom she and my father had socialized. She argued and split with a family friend, a widower who had taken up with someone younger, beginning a new family even as his old one crumbled from neglect. Still, we sensed she was restless. The very air we breathed supplied us with our foundation: A nuclear family had to be paternally secured. We felt the town's watchful eyes. We felt the change coming. And, of course, change inevitably came, first with Don, the odd divorcé in town, and then with Bernado, a married out-of-towner. It came and stayed until fidelity and adultery themselves promised a kind of stability.

From the beginning, Don promised nothing and threatened everything. He was clearly not head-of-household material. He was a "diversion" (a new word for us)—one that our mother couldn't or wouldn't be argued out of. Equally baffling was his interest in her. She had been considered a beauty, but that was years and four children before she rallied around her "family is enough" flag, before we even knew her. We had to accept the testimony of others and the evidence provided by amateur photographs and those professional ones that color pastel over black and white. Four grown children later, at forty-five, my mother still had thick, red hair and green eyes, but she was battling a forties spread I now know well, the crowding of the lower teeth, the receding of the jawline, the sagging jowls so typical of aging women in the Machado clan. And there was Don, a mere pup of thirty-nine, handsome, trim, fit—and ridiculous. Those who cut their literary teeth on the *New Yorker* might see in this depiction a typical therapy case: young adolescent girl can't come to terms with her mother's sexuality. But for a rural community, that's urban myth, and this is an aggie story, which means that sex wasn't the problem. Families were made in the backseats of cars and confirmed at the church altar. It was the restlessness that came with it, something even the young in farm communities could ill afford. Their livelihood demanded that springs be brief, summers long. But in those changing 1970s, spring seemed to lengthen. Anything could happen, and something more did. Three dates into the Don affair, Bernado showed up, "an old friend," in San Francisco on business, "in the neighborhood," a mere three-hour car drive away.

If Don had little to recommend him, Bernado had a lot. For starters, Bernado and my mother had been in love twenty years earlier, had been, in fact, engaged to be married. And now they were in love again. I could tell from the glances they exchanged, glances I'd seen only in movies. Bernado brought along a past, a passion ready to spill. And, odd as it may seem, like Katharine's illicit French tryst, the possibility of adultery promised stability for the first time since we were left, suddenly and unprepared, a widowed family.

III

> *Modernism inaugurated a reversal of values which emphasized erotic desire, not love; anarchic rupture and innovation rather than the conventional appeals of sentimental language.*
>
> —Suzanne Clark, *Sentimental Modernism*

So these are love stories, which push the generic edge of the essay's boundaries as we navigate through postmodernism in the new millennium. Narrative the essay can sustain, but something like love? Especially this kind of love, the very goo of women's magazines that seem not to have progressed beyond the slow drip of Victorian sentiment? This essay form that's been celebrated from Montaigne on for its elasticity, is it really that plastic? What of what Katharine White called that "certain masculine detachment," that "virtue" (Davis 1989, 70, 90) she strove for in life and, by extension, in the *New Yorker* reminiscence pieces she edited, those that came to define the modern U.S. essay? In an irony worthy of modernism, Andy "What Do Our Hearts Treasure" White was a sentimental Cornell man; his wife was a reserved, avowedly unsentimental Bryn Mawr woman. The times, perhaps, dictated the pattern. Although White is best known for his ironic humor, his essays, particularly those around and after the Second World War, might be better characterized as attempts to modernize sentiment. While perhaps not dripping with the teary emotion of late-nineteenth-century prose, his essays show other features of sentimental literature—the bourgeois retreat into self, into the inner life, and, conversely, the humanistic impulse to establish sympathetic connections with other thinking, feeling selves (cf. Baym 1998, 337). As a man, particularly as a young man, E. B. White was able to make frequent, unexpected retreats, even to take what he called his "year of grace," a time in which he sought to "forswear certain easy rituals," including work, marriage, and family. His letter proclaiming and justifying his "Year Off" to his wife (Elledge 1984, 200-02) might serve as a defense for the essayist.

As a young woman, Katharine hadn't the luxury to be an essayist. Nor had she the inclination. Her Bryn Mawr education and her own quest for truth had taught her to suspect her Victorian upbringing, with its beautiful, nebulous sentiments. As a retired editor, Katharine wrote garden essays for the *New Yorker*. (They're published now in a volume with an afterword by Jamaica Kincaid.[2]) In these essays, not surprisingly, Katharine practices what she's penned, eschewing the personal and sentimental. As Kincaid (1997) puts it, White reveals "herself only as she was in the garden; so passionate, but again only as she lived the life of a gardener" (357). It's all we'll ever see of Katharine White's passionate side. Despite flashes of nostalgia for New England girlhood, her pieces remain safely tethered in the horticultural and botanical language of gardening catalogs. She left sentiment to Andy.

Which, to me, though understandable, is sad enough. But there's more: It's this detached voice, this antiengaged view, that has ridden the binary code into the new millennium. For a time, to be sure, in the 1950s, the majority of the *New Yorker*'s readership consisted of suburban, leisured women, but Tom Wolfe (2000) exposed the magazine's "whichy thicket" (273), its embedded relative clauses and womanly curves, and flushed the magazine out from it. Still, what feminine style (and experience) Wolfe picked up on was only faintly etched on paper; *New Yorker* prose merely stood in relief to the manly, modernist literary style in vogue. Katharine White can be (and has been) accused of many things, but overt sentimentalism and girliness are never among the charges. During her years at the *New Yorker*, Katharine, along with celebrity editors like Scribner's Sons' Maxwell Perkins, helped to blue-pencil a detached, "masculine" voice straight into U.S. letters, where it has remained, to spite Wolfe's claim, the essay's sine qua non. The speaker of an essay, writes Phillip Lopate in his influential introduction to *The Art of the Personal Essay* (1995), "must above all be a reliable narrator"; essayists must earn the reader's trust. Such trust, he continues, "issues, paradoxically, from their exposure of their own betrayals," linked to the "insensitivity that wounded another, a lack of empathy, or the callowness of youth" (xxvi–xxvii). While "some vulnerability is essential to the personal essay," the form involves "rough handling," which "begins with oneself": "There is a certain strictness, or even cruelty at times, in the impulse of the personal essayist to scrape away illusions" (xxvi). Lopate's introduction, an important addition to essay criticism, demonstrates that even postmodernism, with all its unsuppressed huffing and puffing, couldn't topple the detached, worldly wise White voice. Indeed, if postmodern has accomplished anything, it has made the accepted voice of the essay, that voice of Tomorrow, even more detached and more masculine, swelling to hyphenated, hopped-up-on-testosterone, rough, cruel ranges. Can an essay or a piece of creative nonfiction survive, thrive, without Katharine's detached, masculine voice? Can it engage sentiment without falling under the weight of a weepy female voice? Without being served up as some kind of chicken soup? Or will criticism keep the essay, the widely touted most protean of protean literary forms, in check, making it impossible, as Suzanne Clark (1991) suggests, "to talk about women writers and the sentimental without eliciting the modern response," that "knee-jerk reaction without parallel in literary criticism" (11)?

We've turned the millennial wheel and are deeply into the rhetoric of new, terroristic, technological times. Perhaps this manly, expansive form can stand just a little female sentiment, even if it is infused with what one *Harper's* editor calls "estrogen logic." A reading of the seventy-fifth anniversary issue of the *New Yorker* (2000), which featured, among other pieces, Wendy Wasserstein's moving piece about her daughter, suggests that perhaps even this august venue is toying with (returning to?) ways of embracing the sentimental. Perhaps, as it seems in the academy, we really are at the dawn of a new millennium where essay writing is concerned. A few semesters back, I went to hear a lecture by an eminent literary scholar, a theorist. He read from his work in progress, a memoir—not a strange thing for an academic to be doing these days. It began in a detached enough way. There were enough references to *The Great Gatsby*, Booker T., and Du Bois to keep the undergraduates in the audience flipping their notebook pages and dropping their pens. There were enough theoretical framings and reframings to let the scholars in attendance know that he wasn't giving up his literary heavyweight title. But, toward the end, the voice of the piece shifted. And while, granted, the death of his father was presented through the obligatorily detached images—a literary device Phillip Lopate thankfully taught me to suspect—the voice was anything but detached. Dare I say it? It verged on the sentimental. When he finished reading, the auditorium was silent. The undergraduates had stopped rustling their papers sometime earlier. The theorists posed no elaborate questions. The writers didn't workshop the piece. Instead, an audience sat silently in a university hall, indulged in oxymoronically thoughtful sentiment. Manly sentiment.

IV

> *Modernism reversed the increasing influence of women's writing, discrediting the literary past and especially that sentimental history. Women themselves participated in this unwarranting.*
>
> —Suzanne Clark, *Sentimental Modernism*

A few months after Bernado's visit, my aunt was fishing for information. "So you were there. What did they talk about?" I knew she'd already tried to fish my mother dry, thrown her hook into the mirage of details that my mother could condense and evaporate at will: details materialized, dripping with promise, only to evaporate, leaving just the faintest trace, no conviction of fact. While Don diverted us, Bernado unified and strengthened us. I was again my mother's daughter. I offered only the most cryptic leads: "They talked about Grandma."

It was true. He did talk about my grandmother, and even more surprisingly, he did like her. I met my grandmother for the second time when she moved from the East to the West Coast, the result of a much-whispered-about nervous breakdown. It was a move she didn't want to make and made for the worst reasons. She didn't want to leave her people—even if most of those she was still speaking to were in the neighboring cemetery. Every Sunday after church, or at least during the Massachusetts growing seasons, my grandmother took her family to the Portuguese cemetery, where they picnicked and tended the family graves: plucked weeds, fed and pruned roses, trained vines, and planted annuals. It was a ritual that ended when my mother followed my uncle west. My grandmother still visited the graves, but now the neighborhood had changed: a tall fence, capped with barbed wire, surrounded the cemetery, and the low cement base was spray-painted in graffiti. She was afraid to stay, so she packed her pictures, most of people who had lived, but some of coffins and gravestones beautifully tended. She headed west to join us in the San Joaquin.

At first, my parents intended to find a new house with a mother-in-law apartment. But, after a few short months of her staying with us, those plans were cancelled. "The children make me nervous." "Your husband doesn't make me feel welcome." She opted to live alone in a small house—was compelled to, she might have said. She complained constantly, about how lonely she was, about her daughter's failing, about our ruffian upbringing, but mostly, she complained about my father. If my mother had to marry a worker, my grandmother felt, he at least ought to be a good one, good at everything from fixing a TV or repairing a toaster to patching a roof, pruning a tree, or unplugging a drain. All of which he did, but my father could never please. My grandmother believed that she had provided my mother opportunities to better herself and that my mother, despite her beauty, had married her working equal and sealed her fate with children. In response to the announcement of my birth, the third such in three years, my grandmother wrote a short note: "There *is* a way not to have a baby every year." To really feel the sting, my mother emphasized, one had to know that the note was from a devout Catholic.

What I didn't tell my aunt was that my grandmother took up so much of Bernado and my mother's conversation because she was instrumental in their courtship. Of course, my aunt knew this already. My mother and Bernado had first met, it seems, at a dance hall during the Korean War. As part of some war effort to boost morale and rally the troops, my mother would join other young women on a bus ride to the hall, dance the night away with soldiers (heavily chaperoned, I was assured), and return home by bus. Most of the men she never saw again. But Bernado was different. On an extended leave, he became a lodger at my grandmother's house, though whether before or after one of those dances, I'm not certain.

The setup sounded somewhat shady to me and my siblings: a romantic liaison between a young woman and a soldier who lived in her house? We'd seen the movies. Then we saw photographs of a romantic outing Bernado and my mother spent at the shore. There's the classic-looking, late-1940s black car, not new but impressively polished; there's my mother in a Lauren Bacall–type suit, her slim, leggy body reclining into the car, mirroring its curves, or draped elegantly on a large rock with waves crashing in the background; and there is my grandmother in almost every picture, tall, dressed in a light suit, pocketbook clutched firmly between both hands at her waist. Of all the pictures taken that day, only one is of the lovers: a shot of my mother wrapped loosely, relaxed into Bernado's left arm, the car and the bridge in the background. My grandmother took that picture. Their whole relationship unfolded under her solid gaze. Without it, they crumbled, though not without great effort on her part to put them together again.

"Your grandmother was persistent." Bernado, it turned out, loved to tell our family stories. "Your mother had moved to the West Coast, met your father, and was about to be married. I was set to marry May. Your grandmother and I had remained good friends. One night, right before your mom's wedding, your grandmother called me, particularly urgent: 'You've got to stop all this, Bernado. Do something. Go out there. Stop her from marrying that man. You must.'

"Of course, I told her I couldn't possibly do that. She was furious—didn't speak to me for a month." He dropped his head and shook it, looking genuinely disturbed to remember the breach.

"A month? How often were you talking with her before?" I asked, mystified that anyone would find a month's reprieve from my grandmother a hardship.

"I told you," he said, chiding me as if I hadn't been paying quite enough attention to the details. "We were *good* friends. I talked to her almost every day."

"Every day?"

He waved me off—*hopeless*—and continued. "Your mother married your father, and your grandmother started talking to me again. I invited her to my wedding, though I was thinking she'd certainly decline."

She accepted, apparently, all too well. She attended his wedding and, a week later, came for an extended stay with him and May. Bernado was in the awkward position of telling his new bride that his ex-fiancée's mother was coming to stay; he couldn't even say for how long.

"Why didn't you just tell her she couldn't come?" I asked.

He paused. No doubt this possibility had crossed his mind. "I liked your grandmother, and *I* had lived with *her*, and she was finally speaking to me again. I knew May wouldn't be excited about the prospect, but I thought she'd adjust, just as if my mother or her mother had come to stay."

I rolled my eyes, teenager-style. He kept on as if I hadn't.

"May *did* make an effort. But not enough for your grandmother. She left in high dudgeon after only one week. 'This is not the welcome I expected.'" He sounded surprisingly like her when he mimicked her voice. "'Your new bride doesn't want me here. I knew no good would come of this marriage. You should have married Chris.'"

Bernado joined us as we laughed, embarrassed yet again by Grandma's theatrics. "What was she thinking to go stay with you? Amazing."

Then Bernado stopped laughing. He grew serious and looked at my mother, another movie glance. "She was right to come stay with us. She was right on all counts."

None of us were surprised when, the next night, Don, my mother, and Bernado returned from dinner at an expensive, elegant restaurant—Bernado's invitation, Bernado's treat—with the gay divorcé Don fuming childishly, formally vanquished.

V

> *The sentimental acts as a pivotal ground in a battle over literary and moral value.*
>
> —Suzanne Clark, *Sentimental Modernism*

Modernism had suddenly hit—delayed, yes; diluted, yes; but powerful just the same. All the rules we had lived by were qualified, or off the books entirely. My mother grew up Catholic and superstitious, but by 1976, she no longer believed in purgatory or saints' intercessions or divine apparitions or papal prohibitions. While my grandmother was part of a generation that knelt its way up the church steps on Our Lady of Fatima's feast day, my mother was among those new Catholics who wanted our dear lady out of the church. We no longer brought flowers to the Virgin's statue on the first of May. We mocked anything vaguely Marian.

And yet, and yet. We couldn't settle comfortably into modern doubt. Even anti-Marian sentiment couldn't hold, as we learned when my mother's best friend Sunny was dying from a slow, lingering colon cancer. Those watching felt relieved when Sunny slipped into unconsciousness; they dreaded the moments she awakened. Then, a few days before her death, Sunny woke up and smiled. "Don't you see her, Chris? That beautiful woman sitting in the tree outside. I always knew she would be so beautiful."

"Yes," my mother answered. "She's beautiful."

When my mother had finished telling us about it, I asked mockingly, "So you really think she saw the Virgin?"

She gave me that look—left brow arched just so, the look she reserved for uppity or ill-behaved or downright foolish children—and then said slowly, in a low voice, *"Does it really matter?"*

I was looking for certainties in uncertain times. Yet, even when I tried to be flexible, to float with undulating life events, I came up rigid and wrong—as I did after my grandmother's death. My grandmother moved to the West with the stipulation that she be buried back East. When the time came to make the arrangements, my mother discovered that transporting a body from one coast to the other is neither inexpensive nor uncomplicated. "Don't do it," I said, with little respect for the dead. "She'll never know." It seemed an appropriate thing to say in post–-Vatican II times.

My protean mother, however, morphed once again. This time, at least, I didn't get the look. Instead I got superstition, which is a kind of faith. "If it's possible to haunt," my mother laughed, "your grandmother will."

And so, in late-twentieth-century America, out of fear of spooks, our family had a body transported back East, to be placed where she could rest, rather than wander or shriek or, worse still, meddle. As if to compensate, when my mother died, she left instructions to be cremated and (postmodernly) scattered.

When I look back at such shifting years, I realize that, for all of the stories told and retold upon Bernado's return, one thing remained unspoken: the act that drove him and my mother apart in the first place. It was no tragic, cinematic miscue but an act of betrayal, simple and classic. When Bernado left my grandmother's house to return to active duty, he left for my mother and grandmother the promise of upward mobility, the hope of marrying up. As my mother soon found out, though, while on active duty Bernado was very active indeed, carrying on most actively with his superior's wife. It was an indiscretion that my grandmother, with her modern, worldly ambitions, could forgive (*men in the heat of battle, fate looming large, the terror of imminent death*). What for my grandmother was indiscretion was, for my mother, cardinal sin. For six months after breaking off her relationship with Bernado, she lived with her mother, becoming, in nineteenth-century romantic heroine fashion, increasingly wan and weightless, until modern times caught up and named the illness "colitis" and diagnosed its roots as "nerves," a popular diagnosis, E. B. White's letters teach us, in mid-twentieth-century America. "I never realized nerves were so odd," wrote White in 1943, "but they are. They are the oddest part of the body, no exceptions. Doctors weren't much help, but I found old phonograph records are miraculous. If you ever bust up from nerves, take frequent shower baths, drink dry sherry in small amounts, spend most of your time with hand tools at a bench, and play old records till there is no wax left in the grooves" (246–47). Ten years after E. B. White's attempts, my mother found her own cure. She moved to the West Coast, as far away as she could get from her troubles—both of them.

When Bernado returned after twenty years, my mother was not looking for an affair to remember. Instead, she was gathering her children around her in an act of self-definition. Her life had not ended in betrayal. She had been fruitful and multiplied. Her children would rise up and call her blessed. (Bernado and May were childless.) It was vindication, pure and simple. Only it was bound to backfire because she wasn't by nature vindictive. Furthermore, the happy family unit so necessary to vindication was starting to unravel after her husband's death. What's left in the face of such realism but religion or romance? She had tried religion, but when the church experienced its crisis in authority, she defaulted to romance.

And so it was that she and we were seduced into a decade-long affair with a married man. He continued to live on the East Coast, she on the West. A few weeks here and there, she met him for trips at mountain lodges, in romantic cities, at trendy spas—trips from which she returned radiant, beautiful. It was also a family affair, destined to carry me to the *New Yorker*'s world. I made my first airplane ride to New York City to visit Bernado. We stayed at an old hotel within walking distance of Radio City Music Hall. He took us to see the World Trade Center and the Statue of Liberty, to Little Italy for dinner. One night, he gave my sister and me—both over eighteen now—cab fare to get from the music hall to our hotel. We pocketed the money and walked to the hotel, staying close to the crowds on the street. A real blood father couldn't have been angrier. "You did what? Don't you know that's not safe? I see I can't leave you two alone again." And he didn't. For the rest of the trip, he was our constant escort. We overlooked the fact that, the other fifty or so weeks of the year, we traveled unescorted. We didn't talk about the fact that he was married to someone else. We fantasized a family, whole, unassailable, protected, our father rich, our mother good-looking. It was a beautiful family, the one my grandmother dreamed into being. For ten years we continued that family affair, that powerful maternal legacy created and sustained by my grandmother, who now lay in a family plot overgrown and untended.

Now *we* were in most of the pictures. And we weren't nearly so vigilant.

VI

> The spider, dropping down from twig,
> Unwinds a thread of his devising:
> A thin, premeditated rig
> To use in rising.
>
> And all the journey down through space,
> In cool descent, and loyal-hearted,
> He builds a ladder to the place
> From which he started.
>
> Thus I, gone forth, as spiders do,
> In spider's web a truth discerning,
> Attach one silken strand to you
> For my returning.
>
> —*E. B. White, "Natural History"*

Truly, disaster should have struck. But it didn't, or at least not right away, and not in the ways one might expect. Like the Katharine and Andy affair, it was all more predictable than that. Yes, the affair went through the usual stages of fire and fizzle. But after several years had passed, when I'd ask about Bernado, my mother would just shrug, or say "the same," or say nothing at all. While she might have been angry at some point, after a decade she wasn't. Nor was she bored. I could tell by the sexy edge in her voice during their occasional phone conversations. It was just that now, ten years later, the rules had changed again, and what she had with Bernado just didn't fit; in her own words, it "just wasn't enough." The *New Yorker* influence had waned; geographical boundaries had recoiled. We were all about stability now, we were about to celebrate three marriages—mine, my brother's, and hers. Bernado didn't disappear entirely.

But the next time he just happened to be in the neighborhood to propose a dinner engagement with my mother and her soon-to-be husband, she flatly declined. At one point, Bernado spoke of his own remarrying (the object of his affection was a much younger nurse). "You'll never do it, Bernado," she told him (and us). "It involves divorce, and you're too constant. Besides, you're not in love." He wasn't and he didn't. No longer the wan heroine or the distressed widow, my mother was running the show now. Bernado had to take his place in the background. And this held as long as she was doing the directing. But things come along and shape people and their lives, whether they will have them or not. In my mother's case, it was ALS, better known by the man who gave his name to the disease, who raised it from the obscure pages of medical pathology to the high profile of cultural myth. "Fans, for the past two weeks you have been reading about the bad break I got. Yet today I consider myself the luckiest man on the face of this earth." In 1939, Lou Gehrig uttered his farewell address to the newsreel, and audiences wept for their misfortune. Three years later, the country wept again as Gary Cooper recited the same words to end *Pride of the Yankees*, a film that became a classic (nominated for eleven Oscars) and perpetuated the public mourning. Who in this drama is defining whom?

Lou Gehrig's disease is not a disability but a fast, slippery slope of disease, taking, in my mother's case, speech, then swallowing, then breathing, within a year's time. It is a disease worthy of a name with the power of 493 home runs behind it. And it brings with it the weight of sentiment, the raw, attached love I felt for my mother. While to say so outright might send us too uncomfortably close to the world of ladies' magazines and chicken soup, it's a truth that I must stake. Yet there is a kind of sentimentalism I resist, even as I'm making the case for more literary room for it. My mother was twelve years old when *Pride of the Yankees* debuted. She lived sixty-five years without Gehrig's iconic disease and one year with it. Is it possible to pay tribute to her life, to compose, as she did, her first sixty-five years, without that final year that recasts the others into a tragic, weepy script? It's not a disinterested question. Will all my years of living and narrating myself change in the last hour, with one mistake, with one assault, with one accident? Will I have no say at all about how my *whole* life story is told?

Sometime in the last year of her life, my mother said what most people say in such circumstances: "Remember me as I was, not like this." I wanted to comply, but I doubted whether I could ever see anything but this final sight: her with the voluntary muscles of her respiratory system degenerating into paralysis, each breath labored, beginning now in the constriction of her lower throat, rising with her shoulders, finishing with the amplified echo, the loud *shhhhhhh* of the ventilating machine—breathing, which should be done and not seen, now seen and heard, and done badly. On the night before she died, I arrived late to spell my niece, who reported that my mother was agitated, readjusting over and over the mask of her ventilating equipment. My niece had given her a sedative, which was slow to take effect. But, in a little while, my mother seemed to drift into rest, unpeaceful as it was with the Sisyphean labor of her breathing.

Then I saw it: a letter from Bernado lying casually on the table. I assumed she'd already heard it, but I read it aloud anyway, mainly to blanket the equipment's sound with my own voice, but also to conjure different times. I don't remember the exact words of the letter, but his letter did what just minutes before had seemed impossible. It conjured her lithe body, the one he caressed on the dance floor, the one he held at the beach with my grandmother smiling on. For a time, the breathing machinery faded. I knew then why we'd let him in, a married man, despite the watchful eyes of the town. A New Yorker by birth, he was every bit the modern essayist, composing a beautiful woman from a tragic widow. And here he was doing it again, this time magically, movingly, turning Lou Gehrig's tragedy into a love story. What more could one hope for from a lover, from a father?

Certainly, that's got to be enough. It's much more than many people will ever have. But I suspect that my mother, in her latest incarnation, would have pointed to the actions of a traditional grieving husband, silent tears by the bedside and such. As always, I want to figure her out, know exactly what she would have thought, fix her ideas and make them stick. And, as always, I can't be certain, not even now, when her life is completed and whole. I still see the voluntary muscles of her left brow arch in just the right way or hear her voice low and slow and insistent—*"Does it really matter?"*—knowing that no matter what answer I give, her very question makes it relative and unstable. We are still so thoroughly, so helplessly modern: on the one hand, fighting belief and sentiment; on the other, placing our belief firmly in the prediction that science and technology will take us on thrilling rides to virtually new expanses. We hesitate and speculate and worry even as we're carried along.

And yet I know this with certainty: the new millennial electronic age will cause nothing more unstable than did the old "solid" ways of loving and grieving. And if that's too sentimental a point for the protean essay at the dawn of a new millennium, then maybe we're just not ready to essay in it. Writing about late-nineteenth-century sentimental novels, one literary critic reflects that "sentimentalism is what remains, or becomes possible, only when everything else has been lost" (Baym 1998, 349). Maybe our cultural memories are too short, too feeble, to remember what we lost in the last millennium or even in the last decade. Or maybe we remember, but we don't allow ourselves to feel it, and this distant, detached stance is our late-twentieth-century contribution to literary history: a cold war, a cold people, a cold literature. We are essaying with all our new technologies in our new millennium, but we can expect the same old, unsure voice to repeatedly greet us, unless we're willing to detach occasionally from detachment and irony—to engage loss and employ the depth and gendered range of sentiment.

About five years after I wrote "Modern Fidelity," I went to visit my aunt and uncle, who have moved back to Massachusetts. My aunt is the truth teller in our family. I'm afraid in her presence to narrate any family story that I think I know, because I know it's coming—some correction, not of a small point, but of the point that drives right to the heart of the story. I didn't think "Modern Fidelity" was at risk; I felt on solid ground with this one, until I did the Parker Street tour with my aunt and uncle. It was one of those "what used to be" tours, where everything is identified not by what currently stands, but by what was once there. "There is where your grandmother lived, where your mother and your uncle were born." The houses were all tall, but it felt as if I could reach up and open the front doors from the sidewalk. In the West, the Midwest, and the South—all places I've lived—the lots are bigger and houses sprawl out. Lot size and house size mean everything. What did it mean to own a house like this one on Parker Street? I couldn't exactly tell, and that bothered me. I somehow had it that my great-grandmother had worked as a companion to a wealthy woman in New Bedford. "That's why we didn't live in the Portuguese ghetto," my mother had told me. "The wealthy woman's husband was a ship captain; he was away at sea. She built a house for your great-grandmother right next door to hers."

I looked at my aunt. I wanted to ask her if the story my mother had told me was true, but I couldn't quite do it. I found a way to ask it safely: "Did Great-Grandma work?" I asked.

"Yes," she said. "She was a housekeeper. You know the antique bedroom set your sister had? It was made for your great-grandmother, when she got married."

There was just no use saying, "I heard the wedding present also included a house, right next door to the big house." The evidence of the tall houses, all pretty much the same size, the proximity to the street, and the long distance to the ocean suggested that my aunt's version, as usual, was right.

After Parker Street, we visited the Portuguese cemetery, where my grandmother and her parents remain. I had expected urban blight—graffiti, barbed wire, a vague sense that our safety could be threatened at any moment—but there were no such signs. And, although I saw many Portuguese gardens in the surrounding neighborhood, the cemetery hadn't any. *Just details*, I told myself. So Grandma didn't move west because she was frightened; there was still the motivation of a nervous breakdown.

Later, in my aunt's kitchen, we got on the topic of Bernado. I don't remember how the topic of the letter came up, but it did. "Oh," my aunt said, "he wrote, then? I'm glad. I called and told him to write, but I didn't know if he'd done it." On the way home, I found myself wondering again and again what the socioeconomics of Parker Street were and whether the cemetery was neatly tended and if my aunt had directed Bernado to write the letter. He wrote it, right? Does knowing that she directed him change the way I felt when I read the letter aloud? The way I should remember and inscribe that moment? A part of me keeps trying to argue, *No, not really, certainly not; same people, same letter.* It's not a terribly convincing voice. I'm left with feeling fortunate that I was able to write "Modern Fidelity" when I could believe.

Notes

1. Information about the Whites' love affair comes from Elledge (1984) and Davis (1989).
2. See also *Two Gardeners: Katharine S. White and Elizabeth Lawrence—A Friendship in Letters* (Wilson 2002).

"Just What the Muscles Grope For"

> *There is no such thing as memory: the brain recalls just what the muscles grope for: no more, no less: and its resultant sum is usually incorrect and false and worthy only of the name of dream.*
>
> —William Faulkner, *Absalom, Absalom!*

My husband eventually read "Modern Fidelity," and he found himself appalled not by my sentiment, but by my lack of it. "Janet," he said, looking at me as if I were a stranger, "what about your dad? How could you represent this other guy so fondly?" My husband and I have been married for over ten years now, so I can understand his anxiety. It's not that I haven't tried to write about my father. I have. But, because he died when I was young (just thirteen), I have few memories. Yes, I could write a profile based on family stories. Or I could write a story about a father-daughter relationship in arrested development. That one is scripted: a textbook study we were—my packet of will, my sharp edges of self-definition grating against him. But that's not the piece I want to write. I want to write an essay about him, in part because I long for the detailed memories. It's a chicken-and-egg thing: I want the details to write the essay, but what I really want are the memories an essay is built on.

After "Modern Fidelity," or rather, after my husband's reaction to it, I wanted to try again to compose something about my father, and so I'm making another stab at it. It's slow going, this essay writing about my father. I'm reaching back into memory, but the pickings are few. I want to work without photographs or family stories. I struggle to make sense of the few impressions that did form, and I grow impatient that they aren't more significant. Why these? Why not others, surely more telling? For example, I remember the breakfast my father made the day my brother was born. I try to make the event meaningful, but given that I'm working with oatmeal, it isn't easy. What made this memory stick? And then I slowly compose some sense: He was home. We were a working-class family, scaling our way into the middle class. Overtime was more usual; Christmas and Easter were the days off. But that morning in 1963 when my brother was born, my father was home, and he fixed oatmeal for three pre- and elementary schoolers, adding too much salt for the "dash" required by Quaker Oats. Naturally, we complained. "Just use more sugar," he said, in the same voice I use when my younger son asks, "What *kind* of oatmeal?" as if there were any choices in my kitchen. That morning when my father fixed the oatmeal, I would have been almost four years old. I don't have many pure memories of him, but this one I am sure of. It rests in my taste buds.

Other memories are fixed in less physical places. They're linked with attitudes, with postures, with acts of self-definition. My father struck me, really struck me, only once, but the memory isn't located in the flesh. There's no pain associated with it. He hit me, but I felt my strength. I had, after all, moved him not just to feel anger (any of my siblings could do that), but to strike me on impulse, something he had never done and didn't want to do. Although we stress the vulnerability of teenage girls—the dangers in the world, the dangers of seduction, the dangers of wrong place, wrong time; the "trouble" girls can find, the unspeakable troubles—thirteen-year-old girls, those somewhat protected at least, feel power, and rightly so. My father struck me, but I pulled together every bit of self I had; I stood and didn't flinch. I was solidly *me* in a way I never had been.

It was I against him. Or rather, I against them. My father somehow always comes through my mother. The day they took me shopping for a winter coat stands out as a bit of cherished dependence in my war of independence. There I was, sandwiched between my parents on the bench of my father's Ford truck—not in the camper, with my brothers and sisters, separated from my parents by a sliding glass cab window and an intercom. I was sitting right there in front, as close to the stick shift as I could get without driving. This was a remarkable event. I was absolutely alone with my parents. We were headed out of town. And to top it off, I was to receive a new coat, not a hand-me-down. I have no idea why I alone made this trip. This I remember, though: My mother selected the coat. It was a pea coat, such as my father might have worn at age seventeen, shipping with the Navy to engage the Koreans. I wouldn't have known a pea coat from a flea market, but my mother was filled with such specialized words—not shoes, but pumps or loafers; not a dress, but a jumper or an A-line; not a hairstyle, but a Gibson girl or a pageboy. I don't remember what the coat looked like—navy blue with anchor buttons, I imagine—but I remember the feeling of trying it on and spinning in the mirror as my parents looked on with admiration, with approval, at my thirteen-year-old body, which made even a navy pea coat look a thing of female beauty. It was an amazing show, an oxymoronic display of confident, oblivious self-awareness, and I was the star.

So I've got oatmeal and a pea coat. I also, of course, have memories of his death. When he died, I was in junior high and obsessed with grief and melancholy—and Faulkner. "Ay, grief goes, fades; we know that—but ask the tear ducts if they have forgotten how to weep" (143) says a character in Faulkner's *Absalom, Absalom!* (1936)—and never, to my thirteen-year-old mind, was the problem more clearly stated. Many of Faulkner's novels are studies in arrested development, studies of loss and reconstruction. "Between grief and nothing," a character in another Faulkner novel ventures, "I will take grief."[1] That was the choice I made—at least then. That was the choice I wanted, even as I knew that middle-class adults in the early 1970s had discovered a whole range of ways, a whole market of talk-therapies, to mediate grief. I didn't want to survive the feeling or talk about it; I wanted to indulge it, to stand in a driving rain, not to take sick or to emerge dry, but just to soak, immerse. To do anything less seemed to me to diminish the importance of a life, my father's life. Sure, it was age (and reading) that drove such a feeling, but it was also culture. My grandmother and her other Portuguese friends wore black and wailed from the back of the church, clutching their rosary beads. My mother had grown conscious in the 1960s. She was New World, not Old. She pulled bright post-Vatican II clothes from our closet and found someone to play a guitar at the wake.

I wanted to wail like my grandmother, but, like my mother, I was more hip than that, so, dressed in creative-writing black, I recorded things—his truck pulling into the driveway just as it had every day (only this time, of course, someone else was driving), the platters of ham and potato salad and doughnuts that filled our refrigerator and spilled into the neighbors', my search for empty space in our neighbor-filled, small suburban California house (euphemistically called "ranch style," although we owned just a patch of lawn in the front and rear). I remember doing this recording—it's important to me—even though I no longer have what I wrote. I recorded everything in pencil and folded the wad of paper not in halves but in fourths, making very few words of the original recoverable when my mother pulled the folded record out of a pile of family treasures ten years later. Since then, I have misplaced it; perhaps I even threw it away. So the words are gone, but it's important to me that I did purely and simply record the truth, as it happened, as it unfolded. I chose grief and made it live. And, though I recognize this as juvenile behavior, I still admire the tenacity and veracity of those lost recordings. It seems that some memories, memories of sacred things—like people—should be preserved in a space of the brain where images and dreams and fictions can't filter through. It's a quixotic wish, a regressive one, but it's why the memory of salty oatmeal, for me, is crucial. I'm certain I neither dreamt, heard secondhand, imagined, nor transposed the salty-sweet taste of over-salted oatmeal. The rest, granted, I'm less certain about.

For instance, here's another memory: my father working in the yard of our sixteen-hundred-square-foot home. Our house, like all the houses in the area, was built on the San Andreas Fault. The sidewalks were uneven, jagged paths: a challenge for feet, let alone skates. We also had a brick patio, one my father laid with his own hands. In the center, he built a wishing well, also of brick. Just like the sidewalks, the patio wouldn't stay level. Every year, he pulled up the bricks again and laid them down, level. One year he tried setting them in sand because he thought it might be more forgiving. It wasn't.

That's the image: my father with the level, laying and relaying bricks. I might know it from watching him, from hearing his impatient responses to me as he worked, from the sense of being unwanted, even as an observer. But, then again, I might know it from my mother, explaining to me after my father's death that Type A personalities are destined for something killing (a heart attack, a stress-caused cancer)—my mother, laying out the moral that it doesn't pay to strive for perfection in an imperfect world. Maybe. Or maybe, I think then and now, it's just plain foolish to build a brick patio on a fault. I could and can draw my own conclusions, and sometimes my own images. Because Faulkner had it right: I "knew it already, had learned, absorbed it already without the medium of speech somehow from having been born and living beside it, with it, as children will and do" (1936, 212–13). I didn't need my mother to lay it out word for word, to wrap his life in layer upon layer of late-twentieth-century sense. I just needed and still need to remember what wasn't articulated.

It's difficult to unwrap, but beneath all the layers of telling and retelling rests this: A level is a neat tool. My dad's had a yellow bubble right in the center, and at the slightest move, it would move off-center, off balanced. In general, he yelled a lot and cursed. He scowled and frowned, leaving deep lines in his broad forehead even at forty years of age, lines replicated now in my own forty-something broad forehead.

Thirty years after his death, I find myself trying to conjure him, but this time the memories, what few there are, surface without Faulknerian heat, without the ability to evoke grief, let alone sustain it. "Between grief and nothing," it seems, I have chosen the all-too-human and adult and middle-class healthy choices that rest in between. Thirty years later, accurate and faithful recording doesn't work; memory is too feeble, the human spirit too resilient, religious faith too strong, the human capacity for art and narrative too entrenched. The very tools of essay writing—memory, accurate recording, doubt—seem to fail. I cannot conjure him, I can only compose him, create him or some idea of him. I can't write an essay about him, only an essay about trying to write about him, another essay about essays, a genre I didn't intend. What I really want, my fantasy of the straight-up, bona fide essay, won't emerge because I can't separate my own memories from photographs and family legends. As important as visual and verbal memories are, I still retain that juvenile conviction that something else matters more, something with more heat.

This weekend, I went out of town for work, leaving my husband and my two sons, ages nine and seven. *If I don't return,* I thought, *what will my boys remember?* Certainly they would carry something of their time spent with me, but it would be carried only partially in the narratives my husband tells or the visual record of family photographs, in those home-movie versions of me. Instead, I imagine that sensations will sustain and carry me, keep my presence in them—the tastes of certain foods, the other-worldly impression of attending a performance, the smoothness of skin stroked, the tension of a hand too firmly grasped, the kinds of "living beside it" experiences that we intuit vaguely, dreamlike, without the presumed accuracy of careful articulation, without the presumed verisimilitude of photos.

"Your illusions," two characters in *Absalom, Absalom!* discover as they piece together the memories that become the many conflicting stories in the novel, "are a part of you like your bones and flesh and memory" (348). I've got the stories and photographs; I've got the illusions: It's the bones and flesh I want back. And, occasionally, I can still feel—things like sitting on my father's lap, not as a very little girl, but as a coming-of-age adolescent, sitting on his lap regressively, as if I were still a small girl of five or six, sitting on his lap, grooming him the way monkeys pick at each other at the zoo, discovering every clogged pore or stray hair that needed attention. I am no longer small, and he is no longer a little girl's daddy, but I can feel again the sensation of sitting on his lap, the comforts of being wholly dependent. I feel it as a moment of flawed beauty, a willing suspension of independence, personhood, a brief lived fiction. It's as close to an essay as I can get, but it feels just like laying bricks on a fault.

Note

1. From the conclusion to *The Wild Palms,* 1939. It's a line I've been drawn to more than once. See Eldred (1988/1989).

Houses II

It is the strangest yellow, that wall-paper! It makes me think of all the yellow things I ever saw—not beautiful ones like buttercups, but old foul, bad yellow things.

But there is something else about that paper—the smell! I noticed it the moment we came into the room, but with so much air and sun it was not bad. Now we have had a week of fog and rain, and whether the windows are open or not, the smell is here.

It creeps all over the house.

I find it hovering in the dining-room, skulking in the parlor, hiding in the hall, lying in wait for me on the stairs. It gets into my hair.

—Charlotte Perkins Gilman,
"The Yellow Wall-Paper"

Our Old Kentucky Home

When we moved with our children and aging in-law from my husband's house into the house that became ours, it was I who delivered tirades against the walls. For the first time, I understood how overwhelming it is to have someone else's life and choices cluttering one's own. I felt compelled to strip the wallpaper, pull up the carpet, and paint more neutral-colored walls. I had to rid the house of them, the house's second owners, in order to make the place ours. It's been something of a failed project: Six years later, I still push in the year of their anniversary—

1936—to quiet the alarm that we don't set and don't understand. Sometimes, usually inconveniently, in the wee hours of the morning, the alarm shorts into a loop, and we have to enter *1936 1936 1936* over and over, until the circuit reconnects and restores silence. Their anniversary date comes almost as readily as my own. And, six years later, old towners still refer to our house by the old owners' name. I feel it most acutely when I give directions to anyone who's lived in town for more than a decade. "Go through the light; follow the curve in the road; it's about seven houses down, a stone house." I see the puzzled look, give in, and start Kentucky speak: "We live in the Pauls' house." "Oh sure," they say, "I know it," and the inevitable, "Why didn't you just say so in the first place?" The outside address, the associations, the alarm that's intertwined with the smoke detector and the telephones (cut one cord, cut them all) I can probably never change, so I had to change the walls, the inside.

There were other matters more pressing, as the inspection report reminded us. There was an "atypical" crack in what looked like the foundation, and the roof was "at the end of its useful life." There was also the issue of lights. The house had a few overhead lights—four in the kitchen, several in the basement—but none in the living room, den, dining room, or bedrooms. Antique wall sconces had once been in the house, supplemented with antique torchère—not "antique" as in Aunt Margie's Country Store, but the real deal, shipped from places like Paris and Austria. We never saw the beauties—they had been removed for auction before we saw the house—but rumor has it they were exquisite. Our whole house, in fact, had been quite impressive. It represented a way of life still dimly lived on our block.

In 1931, the house that would become ours consisted of a story and a half: On the first floor was a small kitchen, a dining room and living room for entertaining, a den, and a bathroom. Upstairs was the only bedroom, a small attached nursery, and the bathroom. Sounds simple, but there was nothing simple about this house. It was typical of the houses built by people who had money during the Depression. My father-in-law, now in his late eighties, a welder by trade, lived during the Depression and loves to tell stories of everything one could buy for a nickel. "But who had a nickel?" he always asks rhetorically. He did not. The people who built this house had a nickel—and a few dimes besides. The neighborhood is reminiscent of the lives one reads about in the early days of the *New Yorker* (which seems to have largely ignored the "downturn"), the kind of lives spoofed by Patrick Dennis in *Auntie Mame* (1955):

> The Upsons lived the way every family in America wants to live—not rich, but well-to-do. They had two of everything: two addresses . . . ; two cars, a Buick sedan and a Ford station wagon; two children, a boy and a girl; two servants, man and maid; two clubs, town and country; and two interests, money and position.
>
> Mrs. Upson had two fur coats and two chins. Mr. Upson also had two chins, two passions—golf and business—and two aversions, Roosevelt and Jews. (186)

The owners of our future home were young, so they didn't have it all—at least not yet. But they certainly had a good deal of it. The house, designed as a honeymoon cottage, backed up to a private club, exclusive in all the ways such old clubs can be.

The long, narrow bedroom upstairs, with its three windows looking over The Club (as it's called in our neighborhood, as if there could be no other) and its golf course, came complete with a maid's bell—the maid's quarters were in the basement. The only bedroom had a small attached nursery, with a narrow door allowing passage between the two, and a dressing area with built-in closets with custom drawers and shoe racks. On top of the closets were high cabinets designed specially to hold hatboxes. The dressing area featured a built-in vanity, complete with two mirrored cabinets. One entire closet under the eaves was cedar lined; the other under-eaves closet had a hidden entrance, one of three such hidden closets in the house (furs were stored in one, we were told). The upstairs bathroom was small by modern standards, large by 1930s ones, featuring a shower complete with a sit-down tile bench and six knobs to control the direction, flow, and temperature of the water. It all still works perfectly.

The honeymooners stayed a few years, until their first child was born, and then sold the house to that other young couple, the ones married in 1936. They stayed forty-eight years. He worked as a businessman; she organized their social life. I detest the phrase "lady of the house," detest it especially when it's used now, when it should be thoroughly outmoded. Still, it's the best, the only, phrase I have, even with its modern, belittling assumptions, to describe the forty-eight-year relationship between this woman and her house. This house was her canvas, her clay, her medium for self-definition and expression (classed, to be sure, but what art isn't?). I inherited her garden as well as her walls, and each spring and fall, as I clear still another hidden garden, eradicate yet another patch of poison ivy, or try to, I learn much about what Kentucky climate can and can't sustain. I admire her art, or the traces I see. I learn from it. But I needed to live in my own vision, to do that delicate dialogic dance; restoring, yes, but also creating.

By the time we bought the house, it was quite shabby, which was why we, two professors and a retired welder, could afford it. Stripped of its glory, it sat on the market for a year until we ventured in. It was interesting to imagine our house with expensive Paris antiques—and illumination—interesting to imagine her with her artist's eye stalking the markets, selecting just the right piece to dramatize this corner or enliven that wall. Imagining its former grandeur was what we were reduced to. We were in the dark, particularly in the three main rooms (living room, dining room, den), paneled in three-quarter-inch cherry accented by a walnut floor. We shuddered to think of others who might have come into such lovely darkness and forced light through paint or demolition. We relied on the few floor and table lamps we owned to provide illumination, but, having had light at the flip of a wall switch in our 1990s house, we hadn't acquired many. We needed an electrician more than we needed paint or paper or resurfaced floors.

We also needed to do something about the heat. The part of the house built in 1931 was solid and tight and warm, but the 1957 addition showed all the arrogance of the times. We were a world power; we had energy to burn. As their family grew, the second owners doubled the size of the house to four thousand square feet and added another heater. We inherited the problems of that worldview. The addition was built on a concrete slab. There was no insulation in the roof. The back wall was made entirely of glass doors: 1950s, thermally oblivious glass. No door separated that room from the kitchen or the living areas, making that addition a black hole for heat. The previous owners hadn't cared for two reasons: They were usually in Florida during the winters, and they apparently had money to burn when they weren't. While we were secure and happy in our professorial jobs (blessedly tenured in very tenuous tenure times), we hardly had money to burn, especially since we had yet to sell my husband's house. We were cold, very cold, that first year. We shivered all the more when we opened our heating bills, shocked to see that we were using so much energy for so little comfort.

A solid foundation, a tight roof, light, and heat—they should have been any rational person's priorities. But they weren't mine. I knew what I had to do immediately: I had to redo the upstairs walls and floors. The walls had last been painted in 1957, a powder blue now turned dirty blue. It had been an economical paint job: trim, window sashes, hardware, ceiling—everything was painted the same canary blue. And to match? Carpet. Blue carpet, thankfully not shag. Yet shag or no, I could not sleep one night in that dirty blue sea, that angry cloud of a room. The upstairs had belonged to the family's daughter, and once she had grown up and out, there hadn't been much cause for the old folks to venture up. The neglected walls and floors told the story. Because we turned the first-floor master over to my father-in-law, this original master suite, with all its blues, was now to be ours. Our children would occupy the nursery room next door—also completely blue and grimy, with long, gaping cracks in the plaster. Alyosha, who had grown accustomed to his ultra-cute Dalmatian border, took one look at his walls with fissures a few centimeters wide, and cried. Untenable.

We know that houses tell stories, that they delineate character, fuel or reflect plot events. Poe made the device work in several of his gothic tales. Dickens made the wind whistle through Bleak House and Chancery and Mr. Jarndyce's troubled mind. Charlotte Perkins Gilman's story "The Yellow Wall-Paper" (1892), a classic text in women's studies, ranks with the best of these house tales. It's the story of a woman driven mad by her suffocating marriage and the prescribed standard rest-cure. Her husband John, a doctor, rents a summer house and places her upstairs, where the "paint and paper look as if a boys' school had used it" (43). Her descent into madness is narrated through her reactions to the paper and her husband's reactions to her: "He laughs at me so about this wall-paper! At first he meant to repaper the room, but afterwards he said that I was letting it get the better of me, and that nothing was worse for a nervous patient than to give way to such fancies" (44). Her husband is "practical in the extreme. He has no patience with faith, an intense horror of superstition, and he scoffs openly at any talk of things not to be felt and seen and put down in figures" (41). Her husband also "hates" for his wife to "write a word" (44). He "laughs" at her, but as she explains, "one expects that in marriage" (41).

I think I half-expected my husband to react like John, but he didn't. Before we slept that night in our upstairs room, I ripped up the carpet and its padding made heavy by its accumulated years of mold and dust. That job took about two hours. The next day, and each day for two weeks following, my husband helped me pry the tiny carpet tacks from the ash. He helped me peel the paper and clean the walls and web and spackle the crevices. We worked together until our DNA melded into those walls and that floor so thoroughly that even the most expert of experts couldn't separate the strands. Once the cracks were mudded, he sanded them until they were smooth, and he accepted my choice of mocha brown for the wall color. We painted, then repainted when I realized after we were done that the ceiling needed to be a lighter color for a lifting effect. He did all of the oil-based painting of the off-white window trim and the Shaker-blue baseboards and molding, because I couldn't tolerate the smell. I washed and ironed the muslin curtains and dyed the tiebacks. Yes, the downstairs was cold and dark, but upstairs, we were in home-improvement heaven.

Paint and caulk and spackle are relatively cheap, and the labor, of course, was free. But the floors were another matter. We'd never run a sanding machine, and, wood lovers that we both now were, we didn't want to risk irreparably gouging the ash, so dear a wood. So, despite the fact that we hadn't yet sold my husband's house and were paying two mortgages, despite the facts that we had little light or heat, the roof leaked, and we hadn't a clue about what caused or was causing the crack in the foundation, we went for broke and hired someone to sand and polyurethane the floors. And, though we were perhaps on shaky ground, we knew we'd made a solid decision. Where once there was a rush of dirty-blue adolescent longing, a constant aching for what never was, there emerged rooms that were beautifully and confidently ours, light ash floor gleaming, mocha-colored walls, off-white trim, a ceiling perfectly and clearly delineated and lifted by us out of an ambiguous downward slope. We changed our minds and moved our boys downstairs, next to the in-law suite. We kept the upstairs for ourselves.

Over the six years we've lived in the house, we've continued to work on it, to dream of what it might become. Our house will likely be a project never finished. The roof is tight now, except for the flat area, a 1950s addition that still leaks and apparently always will. In this house, we are the antithesis of what we had before, either singly or together. I hailed from that 1960s-built California ranch home, sixteen hundred square feet, three bedrooms (four children), two baths, and a wishing well bricked from the plans of a ladies' magazine. My husband was raised with his parents and maternal grandparents in a two-story, nineteenth-century home on Staten Island. His grandfather built the stairs in that house. Both of our working-class family homes were more solid than my husband's 1980s-built postdivorce resort-retirement home (the front door blew open when it contracted in subzero weather), but none was as solid as this one, even though we've never fixed the crack. Some structural engineer along the way explained that the crack, located in a retaining wall, doesn't affect the foundation. The wall apparently cracked from the top ("that's good"), from water flowing, the damage presumably as done as it's going to be because the water has now taken another path.

We're not worried. We understand how something can push unbearably just below the surface, and thus we appreciate just how strong that wall is. It has sustained over seventy years of pressure; it's had the whole weight of water constrained, a hard Kentucky rain drawn underground, advancing against it. Now, sometimes in the spring, leaves sprout in that crack. It is atypical, but the wall is strong, alive, and, yes, beautiful.

Neighbors

> *There where it is we do not need the wall:*
> *He is all pine and I am apple orchard.*
>
> —Robert Frost's neighbor classic,
> "Mending Wall"

When I first saw her, a few days before we moved in, with her clearly authentic fur coat and gloves and hat and shoes and Chanel bag just so perfect, looking, at seventy years of age, so old-style, so elite Kentucky country club, I knew in my smug academic heart that I would not like her. I surveyed the neighborhood: a surgeon and his wife next door, with their gate open to The Club and an SUV with a Lexington Lacrosse bumper sticker; a row of large houses being renovated to make them larger still. Within a week, a neighbor several doors down let me know that all the children on the block went to private schools, either one of the two wannabe prep schools or the Catholic school with the right address. It was then that it dawned on me that, after ten years in Kentucky, I was now deep in Bluegrass territory.

We had moved to the neighborhood in part because we had heard good things about the public school, one complete with, of all things, a wonderful little bird sanctuary sitting on the space of the old principal's house—prime real estate devoted to a bird-loving dead principal, love of history and of place so quirky and beautiful it makes one yearn to be a Kentuckian. We knew it was a neighborhood in transition, some older folks living out their retirement in homes they'd occupied for four decades or more, and some newer families, like us, moving in, displacing the old guard, renovating houses past recognition, with little regard for the lives those walls had sanctuaried. Committed preservationists, we vowed to safeguard what we could of the house, even as we made changes to try to make it accommodate us and our lives. Yet, as we prepared to move in and met neighbors in snatches of conversation, or just spied a glance of a hat or a pillar or a fur coat, I was convinced we had made a huge mistake. I heard more details about The Club—"exclusive" in the way Carl Sandburg hated. I found myself determined to dislike the place and the traditions inhabiting it. I would live in this place, but I would not be part of it. I built a wall separating my ethical and political world from theirs.

Almost as soon as we moved in, the neighbors next door began shaking me down. On moving day, they brought us dinner, a home-cooked one, flavored with herbs from the kitchen garden. Several months later, when Alyosha's bitten fingernail swelled and turned a suspicious red, this same neighbor looked it over, pronounced that something had to be done, and promised to send her doctor-husband over to us after he completed his rounds. At nine in the evening, long after we had figured he'd reneged (he had, after all, been volunteered), he knocked on our door, clearly exhausted from a long day's work, and just as clearly committed to checking this one last case. We let him in the dark, cherry-paneled living room, ushering him over to the one floor lamp. He must have thought us gypsies camping in the grand neighborhood, but squinting in the scarce light, he confirmed his wife's astute diagnosis—serious infection that needed to be treated. He prescribed antibiotics, calling the order into the neighborhood pharmacy. By morning, the swelling was down, the redness reduced. We were grateful; we still are. They bring a gift over every Christmas and share plants from their garden. We forgive the lacrosse balls that rip through our newly repaired screened porch. We find their dog when she escapes from the yard. Overall, one can easily see, the generosity scale tips in their direction. We are neighbors, but they are better at it.

So about one household, I could, I had to, accept that I was wrong. I didn't, however, have to admit that I was wrong about the whole neighborhood, that I, too, am narrow and rigid, practicing my own brand of exclusivity. Then the lawyer-neighbor to our right, the one nursing his mother with Alzheimer's, befriended our children and forgave us immediately when a pound dog we had adopted bit his beautiful and beloved spitz—not just any dog, but a gentle thing he had inherited from his daughter when she left after high school.

Eventually, we discovered that the neighborhood, with some exceptions, even had a sense of humor about its own pretensions. In the vacant house almost directly across the street from us had lived the street's poet, Rufus, a man who composed pointed doggerel about his neighbors.

Buy me a bid to the Ball, Mom
Part with a bundle of pelf.
Buy me a date of my own, Mom
I sure want to get off the shelf.

I want to display all my lines, Mom,
For boys who are loaded to see;
So cough up five hundred in cash, Mom,
Or I fear an old maid I shall be.

A filly must show in the ring, Mom,
To bring a fair price at the sale;
So I, too, must show at the Ball, Mom,
To be bought by an opulent male.

I may not be gifted with charm, Mom,
My blood may be thin, but it's blue;
So buy me what every girl wants, Mom,
A glamorous Lester Lanin debut.[1]

Rufus spoofed our neighbor's South-shall-rise-again columns long before I came along. He had his way with the screw-tree topiary that our house's former owners cultivated (something we consciously didn't preserve). For these spoofs, he was loved and valued and lauded as the neighborhood bard.

I was the only one not smiling. We moved into our house in October of 1997, less than a year after Sanya's adoption and my mother's death. My older son was five, my younger son three. My live-in in-law was aging, his mild dementia growing more pronounced. I was drained, exhausted, and, after a preview of the neighborhood, embittered, overwhelmed by blue walls and blue blood.

We'd been in our house just a few days when one of the boys next door, several years older, introduced my young children to "Scottie," a.k.a. the woman impeccably dressed in hats and furs. They came back elated. "She loves kids," my elder son said. "She gives out suckers." I had a vision of Chanel and suckers, suckers stuck to Chanel. This could not be good.

Each day thereafter, my older son, sometimes alone, sometimes with his little brother, walked two houses down to receive his sucker. Soon they called from Scottie's to ask if they could stay and color, or stay and have a snack, or stay and watch television. After five full straight days, I figured Mz. Scottie, as my children came to call her, had probably had enough. "Not today," I said.

"But she likes us," they pleaded.

After a break of several days, I allowed them to go back. Then I insisted they take a few days off. "Don't overstay your welcome," I instructed, an opportunity to teach them a new idiom.

A few days passed, and I received a phone call. "I miss your boys," she said. "Please send them."

They missed her too. So I sent them, that day and every day. I found myself sometimes with a half-hour or an hour free. I worked on the house. I read. I wrote. I took naps. As their relationship grew, they started running errands with her, going to the grocery store, to the dressmaker, to visit her friends. Then I had several hours free, whole afternoons. I took myself to lunch. I found myself delightfully shopping, not for groceries, but for jewelry and perfume, shoes and handbags, out-of-my-reach things that I'd forgotten I liked.

"She's like our grandmother," my children said. They made me buy "pimmena" cheese and crackers, the kind Mz. Scottie bought. They showed me how to prepare the snack, how to clean up *before* biting into it. They played outside on her perfectly manicured lawn, right next to the espaliered apple tree. They parked in her husband Sam's chair, changing his golf channel to cartoons. As her guests, they were permitted this privilege, and he, while grumbling, obliged. They were allowed to use the ice machine on the refrigerator door. Occasionally, they were invited to dinner, for which they got to plan the menu and light the candles. I made them tuck their shirts in and wear belts, though none of this mattered, they assured me. They told me how each day Mz. Scottie put a light kiss on their cheek, "right here," they pointed, as if they could still feel it. For the first time in a long time, I felt rested.

From time to time, I exchanged a few words with Mz. Scottie, but we didn't speak easily. In fact, I envied the long conversations my children had with her. I would thank her for having the children over, and she'd return a gracious "I love having them." We'd compliment each other on clothing or hairstyles. I never expressed to her how much she had given me, how important those quiet minutes had been—at least not in words. Later, after she had a stroke, I visited her almost daily at the various rehabilitation hospitals she moved to in the course of a year. I mostly sat while she rested. Sometimes I helped lift her from bed to chair or back. I'd give her brief rundowns on the boys or ask questions about her therapy, but mostly we just sat together. She was her usual courteous self to the staff, forcing her weak voice always to say a loud "thank you" before someone left the room. The lack of privacy was difficult for her, but it was harder still for her to imagine they thought her ungrateful. "They didn't hear me," she said one day as a staff member left the room and her weak voice didn't carry to the door. I could tell it pained her. Only once did she complain, about a facility she should have said much more about (privilege finds its limits quickly in the forgotten world of elder care): "She left me sitting in a chair and didn't put me in bed. I was cold." She was paying handsomely for such care. For the tiniest moment, I saw a flash of anger, maybe fear.

It was perhaps strange that my children spent time with Mz. Scottie rather than with other children. She asked me only once if my kids ever played with others on the block. At the time, it was a simple question to answer: Because they were so small, their world was small—two houses down was about all we allowed. The boys next door were older. Mz. Scottie was the second house down.

Eventually, after Mz. Scottie left our street for the hospital and then for an assisted-living apartment, the answer grew more complicated. My children grew older, of course, and their beat grew larger: several blocks up, several blocks down, several blocks around. They came home each day, excited about new friends they'd made. Occasionally, they'd bring them to our place, although the neighbor kids on the whole had better electronics (our house was dark and "scary," and we had no Playstations or Nintendos, no Internet connection, not even a Gameboy.) We didn't always know what to make of the friends. One, in particular, would walk right by without saying hello. It was unnerving. One day, I was out gardening when he walked right by in his usual way. "Hello," I said, looking up from the weeds, addressing him by name. He just kept walking. I mentioned this to Alyosha, who asked his friend some days later why he hadn't returned the hello. "Oh," his friend replied. "I didn't know that was your mother. I didn't recognize her. I thought she was the gardener."

"So you see," Alyosha said to me, "he wasn't ignoring you." He was satisfied.

I blew. "So it's OK? It's OK not to talk to an adult because you think they're gardeners? Servants seen but not heard? If ever, *ever*, I hear you've done the same . . ." I was at a loss for what I might do, but my sons got the point, especially since they'd already learned the lesson from Mz. Scottie. Ms. Pauline, the housekeeper, told my younger son one day that he couldn't use the icemaker. "I don't have to listen to you," he sassed. When Mz. Scottie heard, she sent him home. I was mortified. An apology and a promise got him back in, but only several days later. The neighbor kid, from a longtime Kentucky family, one of the neighborhood new guard in the big new houses, seemed not to learn Mz. Scottie's lesson and continued never to address me when I was working. Apparently, it's just too much work to distinguish among laborers.

We were surprised, then, when one Easter, the neighbor whose child seemed never to recognize me outside sent over a huge basket from the best old family-run bakery in town. *Wrong again*, I thought. A few days later, I returned their young dog that had appeared in our backyard. "I've brought back your dog," I said. "I was worried it might get hurt on the road."

Maybe she interpreted my remarks as accusatory. I'm not sure, but I didn't expect what unfolded. "I'm glad you're here," she said. "I need to talk to you about your kids." She paused, steeling herself, visibly showing me just how difficult the words were in coming. When she next spoke, the difficulty had passed; her words came quickly: "They come over every day. They ring the front bell. If our son is outside in front, we don't mind if they play with him. Otherwise, he's busy." And then the clincher: "It's not just us. The family around the corner feels the same way. It's been so distressing to us." She paused, and I could see a genuine expression of pain cross her face, as if she'd just volunteered to feed the homeless and discovered that folks without access to showers might smell. "I've prayed about it."

Clearly, her prayers had brought no resolution or peace, so it was that remark together with the pained look that rattled me to speech. "You needn't have done that." I laughed a little; I just couldn't help it. "You could have just called me."

She told me to please speak to the kids. She didn't want the kids hurt by this. "They're sweet kids." They, of course, cried when I later told them.

By the time I walked the several houses home, I was far from neighborly. I fantasized about the dog, really a puppy, dead in the traffic, and then instantly felt bad, because I love dogs. After I told my husband about the conversation, he called his Jewish friend on Long Island and recounted the events, of course from our outraged perspective. "Yea," the friend said, "suffer the little children."

My husband and I grew up playing on town and suburban streets. "Go play outside," my mother would say, and I'd spend the day bouncing from friend to friend or taking a long walk down the canal bank. *We just don't fit into this neighborhood*, I thought. It's all about schedules and memberships. I now felt closer to the old Club than the new Lexington elite, and that scared me too.

It took a few years and changes in the neighborhood before I could discern a more complicated textile, one with more than two threads. My children have discovered others who play without appointments—some Kentuckians, some out-of-towners, children who dart back and forth, simulating war games or digging in the construction sand—that is, children from other families who mow their own yards and send their offspring outside unscheduled. They worry, as we do: "I'm afraid if we play Frisbee, it might land in someone's yard." "I'm tired of dirty looks every time my dog shits. I need a few acres somewhere else."

I heard a radio segment about Libertarians wanting to "take over" a state, to build a political base by bringing likeminded people together in one chunk of electoral votes. I understand the impulse. Yet such places, I think, always end up a little artificial, like the resort-retirement "community" my husband bought into after his divorce; the impulse is utopian, a good experiment, but destined, it seems, to disappoint. Like Rufus, the neighborhood bard, I feel I have a place here, a critical one. When my husband and I fantasize about retirement places—Vancouver or the Saratoga-Sarasota double—our children protest: this is their home, they are Kentuckians, they'd miss their friends. And they have found some good ones, including the tomboy down the street. Her mother is part of a mimosa-serving garden club, open to everyone. The family has three cats and two sometimes ill-behaved small dogs (one bit the mail carrier, twice). In their old Kentucky home, designed by Warfield Gratz, they throw wild Fourth of July parties, during which we raucously watch the fireworks from outside The Club gates. It seems no accident that these folks gave birth to a daughter with audacious red hair. "I like being in your house," my young redheaded friend told me the other day. "I don't know. It's just neat. I like being here."

"Thanks," I said. But what I was really thinking was this: *I like being here too.* And I do, most of the time.

Dreaming Houses

> *"Wendy, sing the kind of house you would like to have." Immediately, without opening her eyes, Wendy began to sing:*
>
> *"I wish I had a pretty house."*
>
> —J. M. Barrie, *Peter Pan*

From the very first, our kids referred to our new place as "Daddy's dreamin' house." It was. Sometimes, I'd catch my husband in the front yard, sunglasses dangling in hand, just admiring the Kentucky River stone and large trees. "What are you doing?" I'd ask, knowing the answer.

"Just looking at the house. I never thought I'd live in a place like this. It's fantastic. It's my dream house."

Moving to the house taught us something, though we didn't learn it right away: My husband and I love dreaming houses. We're at our best when we're doing it. I've always been a house dreamer. During the eight years we looked for a house, I made plan after plan, sometimes in conversation, sometimes on paper. I even found a Kentucky barn I wanted to convert into a house. We got as far as consulting an architect before my husband realized he was way out on an imaginative limb, and that sketch joined the others in a drawer. These days, we dream together, mostly about this house, but also about our next house, our retirement house, still some years away. Once, when I received a job offer elsewhere, I asked my husband, "But what about the house?"

"That doesn't matter, Janet. There are houses everywhere." Houses everywhere—what a notion! That got us dreaming houses all night long.

We've been six years in our house now and have discovered the most unexpected consequence: Our children, as if the condition were genetically unfolding, are now house dreamers too. The older one, being older and perhaps the more imaginative (the jury is still out, though), dreams more and bigger. He draws detailed maps. He has three major plans: his battle island, where all the nations of the world send soldiers to war so that battles never occur in civilian populations; his estate in Russia, where he will provide housing and food for everyone who wants it; and our current house. His plans for our house are elaborate and always, thankfully, involve us. We will live in the in-law suite; his family will occupy the rest of the house. He needs to make it bigger, he explains, so he'll tear down the house they're building next door (they tore down the lawyer's house, and turnabout, in his world at least, is fair play). That space will be an elaborate garden, with a huge pond.

"But where will I live?" Sanya asks, rightly miffed that he's been left out of his big brother's plans yet again.

"Don't worry. I'll build a small house for you and your family."

"It needs to be close."

"It will be."

Sometimes Sanya plans to have "the big house," as the kids call it, and banishes his older brother.

"That's OK," his brother counters, "because I'm going to have an estate, in Russia." There's just no losing in house dreamin'.

Sure, the plans are usually fantastic, but not always. After struggling with a small pond in our backyard for six years (a mosquito hatchery in the summer, a fish cemetery in the winter), my older son suggested that we fill it in and make a planter. We did that project early this summer.

Both boys have planned various bedrooms, moving to the basement, to the first floor, and back again. They are constantly rearranging furniture, even moving it from room to room. The 1950s addition, which we use only three seasons a year, has a slightly different function each year when we open it (it's a room for board games this year). Just recently, Alyosha reclaimed the nursery, turning it into a studious middle-schooler office/bedroom because he can't be expected to share a room with such a little brother; there's two years difference, after all. The basement, under his domain, has become an unacceptable mess. I successfully nixed the idea of the camouflage wallpaper in the nursery-turned-office/bedroom, but was vetoed when I tried to rearrange the furniture. At eleven and nine, the boys are both furniture movers and gardeners. "Adjust the lawn-mower next time," my older son advises. "You're leaving the blades too long." He's dying to run the machine himself; we're fearful of lost limbs. I'm also fearful when they're on the roof with their father, cutting tree limbs and cleaning gutters, but nonetheless, they're there, tools in hand as they climb the ladder.

Dreaming houses has become a family pastime. We do it on vacation, over dinner, while watching television. I know we do it in our sleep. We do it so much we're not even aware we do it. It's one of the ties that bind us.

These are good times—at least for us. We prosper, part of the privileged. Education has paid off for us; we are that rare thing, employed PhD's. We have our children and enjoy their company, and they ours. We are healthy now. Even dementia moves slowly, almost imperceptibly. Though we are always individually and collectively dreaming, longing for more, we don't need more, so every extra feels and is a luxury. There is much we can give away. Such times are fragile. My husband and I know it. We whisper it to one another at night and hush ourselves, as if speaking might break the spell.

Note

1. Reprinted in the *Chevy Chaser Magazine* August 5, 1998, p. 5.

Daughters of the University

It is fall semester, almost midterm, and a fellow tenured faculty member is returning to town and to her classes for the first time since the first week of the term. She is apprehensive, she tells me, about facing her classes again. She's talking to me because I have had a fall like hers, a fall during which my mother died of a lingering illness.

"It's not like the first-day jitters," she emphasizes. "These faces should be familiar."

They are not.

We go back over old ground. "You did the right thing," I assure her. "How could you have been anywhere else?" We talk about how impossible it is at times like these to live in two so completely different worlds. In one, we are daughters, not yet forty, caring for our mothers who will die soon—tomorrow, a week from today, two weeks. In the other world, we are professors, with pride in our records of strong teaching. We know that while the research will wait, the students do not, cannot.

How, we wonder, do we explain to our students, not the duty that children have to their parents, but the exquisiteness of care, of reciprocating stroke by soft stroke what we have expected and received all our lives? How to explain that draft due dates, editing sessions, and midterms have all but been erased by the *drip drip drip* of morphine or the endless *shhhhhhh* of ventilating equipment?

"My undergraduate students gave me a card," she says. "I feel relieved."

"Yes," I answer, "my graduate students gave me a card when my mother died." But what I am really thinking about are the departmental summaries of my teaching evaluations from that semester, the semester we adopted our second son, the semester my mother was felled by ALS. (As a matter of procedure for merit and posttenure review, one member of our department's executive committee summarizes each faculty person's evaluations. Overall, it's a good policy; even the most "disengaged" of colleagues can't completely escape student opinion.) That semester I had two classes, an undergraduate seminar on writing about place and a graduate seminar for first-year teaching assistants. The undergraduates, who didn't send a card, were, in their evaluations, generous to the point of fiction. The graduate students, on the other hand, had mastered the course content. Their evaluations, according to the department summary, were clear, direct, unambiguous—and damning. They noted (accurately) that I was unenthusiastic, underprepared at best, frequently absent (a month's worth to be exact—two weeks in Russia adopting Sanya, two weeks for my mother's death).

I promised myself not to look at the original evaluations and filed them, unopened, in the drawer that holds the record of fifteen years of mostly strong, successful teaching. What could I possibly learn from those evaluations? That the university has no policy for caring for sick family members? That the university doesn't support adoption, offering as it does only "sick leave" for pregnant women who do that "sick" thing of giving birth? That I could, at the very time we adopted a sick child and needed money for travel home, take the federal family medical leave—several weeks without pay?[1]

But none of this is before me now. A grieving friend and colleague is, and such thoughts offer little solace. I search for something else to say, but my second attempts aren't much better. I want to tell her that this thing we are living will not conform to a university bulletin, that we are living drafts-in-progress that will become final, irreversible products, but not under the pressure of the last day to drop or the last day to withdraw. Again, no comfort there.

So instead, I offer her the only timely, practical piece of advice I can think of: I counsel her not to read her semester evaluations—not even the departmental summary of them.

But she's back to her classes now, back to the semester calendar, and she is thinking about that card. I can tell she will read them—and I know that, someday, I will read mine, because we are orphans now, daughters of the university. We are good girls. We fit in our world—or maybe that's just our own postmodern quixotic desire.

Note

1. In 2002, the University of Kentucky's new president, Lee Todd, approved an adoption benefit.

Conclusion

Why Essays?

Remember, anybody who pulls his erudition or education on you hasn't any.
—Hemingway, as quoted by *New Yorker* writer Lillian Ross

Mary F. Corey opens *The World through a Monocle* (1999), her excellent study of race, class, and gender in the postwar *New Yorker,* with this personal account:

> I grew up in a facsimile of the culture represented in *The New Yorker.* . . . I had Capezio shoes, a progressive education, a pearl necklace, and a midget clown entertainer at my birthday parties. My own curiosity about the small but potent piece of postwar America embodied in *The New Yorker* comes very simply from the fact that I am of it and have, for much of my life, been blind to it, because it is my own. (xii–xiii)

Like Corey, I share a fascination with the *New Yorker* as a cultural institution and as a rich repository for academic study. Still, what's striking to me about Corey's prefatory remarks is how much her point of departure differs from my own. While Corey grew up as one subscribed, I grew up in a family with only loose connections to elite book and periodical culture. The *New Yorker* would have been messy in a household like ours—

it comes much too frequently—and its use limited, unlike, say, *National Geographic,* which lent itself to school projects dependent on maps and exotic visuals and geographic facts, and so earned its place inside the stereo cabinet. It's not that my family wasn't committed to education. In fact, both of my parents enrolled in classes once a junior college opened in our small town in California's San Joaquin Valley. Both were, in fact, religious about education. We knew the gospel: We had no inheritance; our futures depended on education. So we thought, so we believed, so we lived. My mother permitted herself the fancy of a real maple, hexagonal Tell City end table that housed our collection of Reader's Digest Condensed Books, each with its deeply colored leather binding (probably faux, but I thought them real) fitting perfectly into the spaces: four books, a wood divider, four more books, another divider. Books were not just part of the furniture; they *were* the furniture, an aesthetic that lasted through graduate school, when I acquired more and more and lined my stairwells and walls with them.

The *New Yorker* wasn't part of my growing-up life. It came later, once I'd left home, sometime between 1977 and 1982, while I was attending a branch college in the California State University system, taking classes I thought would lead me to a career in optometry. Somewhere along the line, I got waylaid by the sciences (chemistry, in my case, though the story in general is familiar to many of us who started premed) and sidestepped into English and into a classroom where a professor, or perhaps an adjunct, held up a copy of the *New Yorker* and said something to the effect of "This is what all intelligent, educated people read," or maybe he or she simply expressed an enthusiasm for the magazine that implicitly expressed the argument and urged membership. Whatever, I bit. I subscribed. Soon, the magazines began arriving. I tried to read them cover to cover, but I could barely interest myself in a single article, perhaps because I encountered the magazine not during its initial "rambunctious, hit-or-miss" Harold Ross period, but during that time when editor William Shawn fashioned the *New Yorker* into a magazine with "a certain very high level of unbroken excellence, to the point where it was sometimes difficult to distinguish one issue from another" (Gill 1997, xxvi). Excellence or no (or perhaps because of its excellence?), I wasn't, in my late teens, able to crack its code. The issues piled up quickly, a solid mirror to my cultural and intellectual boorishness. What I didn't know then, what comforts me now, is that in the magazine's heyday in 1949, only 3 percent of the subscribers were students (Corey 1999). What I did know then was this: I was relieved after a year when my subscription expired.

As life would strangely have it, twenty-some years later, I find myself completely riveted, engrossed, fascinated ("obsessed" might not be too strong a word) with the *New Yorker.* I leaf through, grabbing a profile here or a Talk of the Town item there, hunting out familiar names, like that of my colleague Bobbie Ann Mason, whose piece "Fallout" (2000; on the nuclear plant in Paducah, Kentucky) floored me, or Adam Gopnik, whose *Paris to the Moon* (2000) pieces delighted me. A nonfiction junkie, I rarely read the fiction. And I don't get the art (they still look just like cartoons to me), but occasionally I try, hoping I've at long last found the necessary sense of humor. When I'm done, I recycle the magazine with the newspapers. A glance here, a glance there—it hardly sounds like passion, I realize, such casual, such familiar treatment. So wherein lies my avowed *New Yorker* passion? In its history. In anything having to do with its legendary founding editor, the uneducated, "oafish," "rural rube," the "galoot" Harold Ross (Corey 1999, 2);[1] his elegant, cultured fiction editor, Katharine Sergeant (Angell) White; his quiet, liberal successor, William Shawn; and a still later successor, the whirling *Vanity Fair* dervish Tina Brown. And with anyone related to this cast of characters: Jane Grant, Ross's first wife and cofounder of the *New Yorker,* later responsible for the GI pony version of the magazine that led to its escalating postwar subscription numbers; E. B. White, second husband of Katharine Sergeant who hired the essayist onto the staff; Lillian Ross, who wrote what many believe to be the first piece of modern U.S. literary journalism and who, we learned through her tell-all memoir (1998), was the longtime lover of William Shawn; and Jamaica Kincaid, the novelist (and William Shawn's daughter-in-law) who daringly made her complaints about the *New Yorker* public.[2]

Yes, like Mary Corey, I have become intimate with this publication and its history. For a good part of the twentieth century, the *New Yorker* found itself in the spotlight because it signified both high and highbrow culture. The other, weightier part of that audience formula, of course, had to do with status, and here too, the *New Yorker*'s ideal seemed to materialize in its subscribers: over half owned valuable property, and three-quarters took home incomes well above the national average

(Corey 1999). Although consciously a "class publication"—a term Condé Nast used (Seebohm 1982, 79)—it distinguished itself from other magazines pitched to an elite society (*Town and Country* and *Vogue*, for example), joining the ranks of magazines (*Harper's, Atlantic Monthly*) that included the intelligentsia as a crucial part of their audience formulas. Though academics formed only a small part of the *New Yorker* audience in 1949 (9 percent), most of its readers had attended college for at least four years (Corey 1999).

Maybe it's knowledge of this history, or maybe it's personal experience, but I've never been tempted to take advantage of the *New Yorker*'s education program, to make the magazine a required text at any curricular level, especially at my institution, where the number of first-generation college students is relatively high. If I were to choose a magazine, I'd select *O, The Oprah Magazine*, although finally I suspect that again what piques my interest is the magazine's history, the cultural phenomenon of it and its high-profile founder. Oprah can get large numbers of people talking about words, even in large "lecture" settings; she motivates people to write, using journal prompts printed on card stock sewed into the seam of her magazine. In short, she seems to have achieved what college writing programs struggle to do: use technology to challenge people—large groups of people (granted, mostly women)—to explore new literacies, to improve their verbal lives, to enjoy the benefits and take on the responsibilities of articulation. She's been so successful doing this that she's made money, a lot of money, and she's used that money to successfully create and support publication venues important to her.

Now, I'm not ready to direct a writing program that makes people aware of their "spirit," nor am I ready to sponsor therapeutic, Dr. Phil–inspired class sessions. Rather, I'd like to propose that people who teach composition might do well to engage the *O*-like activities of authoring, editing, and sponsoring. This book project takes up the first of that trio—authoring—exploring these questions: What unique attitudes do we, as teachers of writing, bring to the essay, a form by no means the sine qua non of composition courses, but one we certainly have a long tradition of teaching? What have we learned about the form from teaching, studying, and practicing it?[3] Have we studied and practiced enough?

These basic questions have the potential to be transformative. If we were to compose pieces accessible to college students, first-year through graduate, and persuasive to colleagues (think, to name a few examples, of Mike Rose's *Lives on the Boundary* [1990], Keith Gilyard's *Voices of the Self* [1997], Min-Zhan Lu's *Shanghai Quartet* [2001], Victor Villanueva's *Bootstraps* [1993], or the interludes in Brenda Jo Brueggemann's *Lend Me Your Ear* [2002]; or essays by Nancy Sommers [1992, 1993] or Harriet Malinowitz [1996, 2002, 2003] or Anne Ruggles Gere [1998]), and we taught such texts in our classrooms at all levels of the curriculum, then we would have transformed our own publishing world (professional and pedagogical), in much the same way that Oprah has changed the profile of her bigger playing field, the best-seller list. It may seem daunting, or even a bit precious or sly, for writing teachers to author like this: Are we trying to become creative writers? To sneak in the back door of creative writing? Have we abandoned our field and our service missions? In addressing these concerns, we might take a page from our colleagues who transformed "remedial" writing labs into centers where writing and writers from novice to distinguished are valued and supported.

It might also seem exhausting to add the transformation of existing publishing venues to already overburdened institutional and social missions. Things are the way they are, right? Publication history once again is illustrative: When Oprah started her book club, the idea was downright quixotic. Conventional wisdom, doomsday prophecies about the end of the book as we know it, and solid market trends all predicted that such an idea would fail. Paul Gray (1996) recounted for *Time* the shock the publishing industry felt when Oprah's first pick actually worked:

> Publishers [and writers] began pinching themselves tentatively, wondering where they were. They have known for decades that TV exposure sells books, but experience suggested that doing it successfully was a matter of getting the right author in front of an appropriate niche audience. . . . But now Oprah had altered the equation by pushing a first novel to her massive viewership.
>
> All thoughts that Oprah's Book Club might simply be a novelty or a fluke vanished a month later, when the second recommendation was announced: Toni Morrison's *Song of Solomon*, a phantasmagoric account of a black man's search for his identity and past, first published in 1977. Bingo! Bonanza time all over again (56).

Within a span of a few months, Oprah Winfrey transformed the mass paperback industry with the simple idea that people from all walks of life can—and wish to—enjoy imaginative reading. "Outside of Oprah," noted the trade magazine *Publishers Weekly* in 1998, "the trade paperback list looks very familiar, particularly in the endless ladles of chicken soup for sundry souls or absolutely anything for dummies books" (56). Occasionally, a work of fiction by Grisham or Steel or Clancy dominates the list, but 1998 marked "the first year in decades to see so much fiction so high on the list. The reason, of course, is Oprah's Book Club" (56).

One academic response to Oprah's tremendous success is scorn. The publishing industry, which may have originally expressed elitist intellectual skepticism, quickly changed key: It knew on which side its starchy profit was buttered. Books were selling again, and Oprah's Book Club had made that happen. Paul Gray (1996) summarized Oprah's challenge to the industry: "If Oprah can make books inviting and exciting to non-readers, who are the purists to complain?" (84). Those of us working in composition are rarely burdened with the elitist label of "purist." I know few colleagues in composition who expect (or even want) what Gray's fictional purist wants: "*Ulysses* and *Gravity's Rainbow* to show up anytime soon on Oprah's Book Club" (84). Yet purists we are on other levels: *Composition scholarship must assume traditional academic forms*; *essays must be published as creative writing*; *faculty in composition must study rather than produce belletristic written forms*—all fiats that resemble ungrounded, tenacious rules like *Don't use "because" to start a sentence.* Far from launching some sort of parody, or more likely, some extended scathing academic criticism of Oprah (no doubt possible, no doubt already done), I want to offer her the highest form of praise by imitating her,[4] or rather, since I have neither her magnetism nor her deep pockets (our university balances its books with the kind of part-time, under-compensated labor detailed in our professional literature), I want to borrow some of her strategies and enjoy a tiny fraction of her success.

There are limitations, of course, to such imitation, the biggest of which is that, because I am an academic, my goals and Oprah's necessarily differ. So for me the question becomes, how can we take Oprah's accomplishments—her authorship, editing, and sponsorship models—and make them work for our field? Once the question is framed as such, it becomes almost rhetorical:

Q: As writing teachers, can we produce and publish and support the forms of writing we have historically most frequently taught?
A: Yes, of course.

In fact, it can be argued, we already do so by ordering and authoring textbooks, some of which include essays by our colleagues in rhetoric and composition. However, our traditional relationship with the textbook market barely taps our potential as sponsors (and we are sponsoring and endorsing each time we order an anthology) and ignores, with a growing number of notable exceptions, our own potential as nonfiction authors. Our course anthologies or readers are filled with pieces from magazines and books, an occasional Internet publication, increasingly some student essays. But here's the deal: With few exceptions, someone else—someone outside of composition studies—initially chose to print those pieces, and their varied reasons for publication, like the editors' at *O* or the *New Yorker*, are collectively different from our varied reasons. We can lament that our professional literature lacks the written spark we try to teach, or we can, Oprah-like, begin to transform our disciplinary publications.

In *Composition Studies as a Creative Art*, Lynn Bloom (1998) poses a provocative question: "Why Don't We Write What We Teach? And Publish It?". The question, I think, is a good one, even if it suggests that all composition courses should focus on the production of literary or creative nonfiction. If we look to the essay in its widest sense, the formal possibilities multiply. Although the essay as a category is probably not broad enough to cover a good deal of what is taught in business and technical writing courses, the form still enjoys wide generic range, with powerful revelatory, reflective, and declarative features. The essay is broad enough, for example, to further the social and political concerns of writers as diverse as Julia Alvarez, Wendell Berry, James Baldwin, bell hooks, and Minnie Bruce Pratt, while at the same time allowing personal reflection and aesthetic articulation of the natural or cultural worlds we inhabit.

Essay writing is a relatively new kind of writing for me. I wrote essays in my first-year college composition course, since I didn't test out. Fourteen years later, in 1991, when I was a visiting assistant professor at Berea College, I wrote a short essay as part of a faculty writing group. Although

I have incorporated essays into writing classes since I began as a teaching assistant in 1982, it never dawned on me—it hadn't been part of my training—to imagine my own writing of essays as appropriate professional work. I began seriously experimenting with different prose forms only later, after I received tenure—and only because it became impossible for me to write anything else, which sounds like one of those statements that novelists or poets make. I don't mean it to; my reasons for writing are much more prosaic. I took to the essay because I was teaching an upper-division undergraduate essay writing course, I had one young toddler and a second adoption about to happen, my mother's health was failing, and I was supposed to be writing a scholarly article for Gail Hawisher and Cindy Selfe on issues of ethics and free speech in electronic classrooms. I couldn't get to the library often, and when I did, I couldn't focus on scholarship. My mind was a jumble of mother–kid(s)–teaching. And, strangely enough, even under the pressure of all that life, I was still an academic, thinking about my topic, technology.

In fact, I was thinking a lot about technology. Some months earlier, my mother had lost her capacity to speak as a result of Lou Gehrig's disease. We were using new technology to communicate—e-mail, a telephone relay. I sat down to write Gail Hawisher an apology when it became clear that the promised article would never get written, and somehow, because I was teaching that upper-division essay class, my apology assumed essay form. The essay I wrote was not designed to be the article that I owed her, but I sent it to her nevertheless, knowing that as a friend she would read it and understand why she didn't have the article I had promised.

Gail did read my essay, my odd apology, and she suggested I send the piece to Joe Harris, who was editing *College Composition and Communication* and "looking for different material." I couldn't believe that he might want something as different as an essay (we teach those, but we don't write them, right?), but I sent it anyway. A few weeks later, Gail called back to say that she and Cindy had decided to open a space for it in their collection *Passions, Pedagogies, and 21st Century Technologies* (1999). Soon Joe Harris sent back the reader reports—one positive, one negative—and asked me for a revision. The general question the negative report posed was an excellent one, although naturally I didn't think so at the time, and it has driven a good deal of my work since then: "What does this personal essay have to do with the teaching of writing?" I quickly turned to Bakhtin, who is never far from my academic psyche, to answer the question fully enough to find the essay a home in *CCC*.

The essay cycle that forms the middle of this book is formed of experimental compositions that center on relationships, or sentimental attachments, as I prefer to call them, yet it's important to me that they contribute to academic discussions. In her work on hybrid academic discourse, Patricia Bizzell (1999), a scholar once seen as "anti-expressivist," acknowledges the importance of the form, noting that personal experience narratives make general ideas salient, bring them closer to home, as the expression goes. Personal experience can be used "to add persuasive force to a point by invoking an emotional response from the reader. . . . Personal experience may also be used in a less emotionally charged way, as a source of illustrative examples. . . . These personal examples present shades of meaning more clearly than an abstract description of traits could do" (14).[5] Personal essays have that kind of power, and yet I haven't stopped thinking of that review, that simple, pointed question, "What does this personal essay have to do with the teaching of writing?" My long answer to that question has evolved over the course of writing these essays and contemplating the direction I want at least some of my further writing to take. Here, in concluding, let me offer the short answer: These essays could only have been written by someone in composition studies. I don't consider myself a "creative writer" or an artist.[6] Ask me to choose between my "art" and dinner, and I would choose dinner. Force me to choose between a writing life and a teaching and researching life, and I would choose teaching and research. I have had writer's block, and I have resisted research, but I have never had teaching block, except during a semester when all my work was halted by grief, by loss that eventually takes its place along life's other memories, not buried or diminished, but set aside to be recalled, re-grieved, or ritualized as occasion or culture or personal temperament demands. Grief, relatively speaking, has been an exception in my life. Generally, I enjoy the immediacy and rhythms of teaching and administration. I would define myself as a teacher and an administrator before I would make claims to be a writer. I agree with the assertion Peter Elbow (2000) makes in his title, *Everyone Can Write*—and I think it's an important premise for all of us who teach composition.[7]

Still, I am not a hobby essayist. I think of myself as someone who practices what she teaches, which is composition: its central tenets, its wide generic range, its skilled components, its wonderful details, its powerful effects. As a writing teacher, I instruct others in how to approach writing tasks, how to reflect on topics (thoughtfully, creatively), how to articulate lived experience (one's own, others') as situated in the larger world and in the world of ideas. I write using academic tools, but not to sound smarter; I do it because I think academic discourse allows me to grasp and probe ideas I otherwise wouldn't have. I write using the tools of creative writing, but not for art's sake; I do it because at its best, belletristic prose can make me think and feel and appreciate all in the same moment. As someone who practices composition, I'm grateful for the wide range of discursive tools available.[8] There's another important facet to my essay writing that I think comes directly from my work in composition and rhetoric: I compose out of principles of "answerability," out of an impulse to care about the world and the place I've fallen or pushed myself into, out of the strong Bakhtinian sense that "the only thing left for me to do is to find a refuge in the *other* and to assemble—out of the *other*—the scattered pieces of my own givenness" (Bakhtin 1990, 126). I compose with disciplinary questions at the forefront: When and how might I make my private academic life meaningfully public? How might I use the personal in ways that mitigate the me-myself-and-I syndrome?[9] When should I avoid disclosure and focus instead, more productively and more deservedly, on someone else's lived experience?

I present the essays herein not as a hobby exhibit, nor as a stellar example of art, but rather, as work. They represent a perspective very familiar to faculty in composition, that "dappled discipline," as Janice Lauer (1984) once put it, with connections to literary studies, to the social sciences, to creative writing, to education, to journalism, and to linguistics. Finally, I would argue, this history explains why we should write essays. We should write not because we want to compete with our colleagues in creative writing and not because we're bored by our own academic publications. We should write essays and compositions because we have a long tradition of teaching them, we have studied them deeply and have admired them, and, because of this academic and creative work, we have a distinctive perspective to offer and a beautiful form through which to explore our deep-seated, dappled, disciplinary thoughts.

Notes

1. I've borrowed from Corey (1999), although these descriptions might have come from any number of books, including Brendan Gill's *Here at* The New Yorker (1975, 1997), Jane Grant's *Ross,* The New Yorker*, and Me* (1968), Ben Yagoda's *About Town* (2000), Thomas Kunkel's *Genius in Disguise* (1995), Scott Elledge's *E. B. White: A Biography* (1984), and James Thurber's *Years with Ross* (1959). Kunkel's edition of Ross's letters offers a corrective to this view and instead paints Ross as a prolific, highly competent letter writer.
2. For a sanitized overview, see the *Salon* feature http://www.salon.com/05/features/Kincaid.html.
3. Some good starting points are *The Encyclopedia of the Essay* (Chevalier 1997), *Literary Nonfiction: Theory, Criticism, Pedagogy* (Anderson 1989), *Essays on the Essay: Redefining the Genre* (Butrym 1989), *The Essay: Theory and Pedagogy for an Active Form* (Heilker 1996), *What Do I Know? Reading, Writing, and Teaching the Essay* (Forman 1995), *The Art of the Essay* (Fakundiny 1990), *The Essayistic Spirit* (de Obaldia 1995), *The Politics of the Essay: Feminist Perspectives* (Boetcher Joeres and Elizabeth Mittman 1993), *Writing Creative Nonfiction* (Forche and Gerard 2001), *The Art of the Personal Essay* (Lopate 1995), *Those Who Do, Can: Teachers Writing, Writers Teaching: A Sourcebook* (Root and Steinberg 1996), *Personal Effects* (Holdstein and Bleich 2001), and *The Observing Self: Rediscovering the Essay* (Good 1988). To this list, I add the volumes narrating (personal) teaching lives: Wendy Bishop's *Teaching Lives* (1997), *Narration as Knowledge: Tales of the Teaching Life*, edited by Joseph F. Trimmer (1997), and Richard Haswell and Min-Zhan Lu's *Comp Tales* (1999).
4. Elizabeth McHenry shares my enthusiasm in *Forgotten Readers: Recovering the Lost History of African American Literary Societies*, 307–315.
5. Bizzell (1999) lists traits of hybrid academic discourse she gleans "from successful, published academic discourse that nevertheless takes hybrid forms" (16). Her list is illustrative rather than exhaustive in purpose.
6. Some in composition and rhetoric have, of course, argued for just such an identity. See particularly work by Wendy Bishop (1997).
7. Donald McQuade also makes the point in "(Re)Placing the Essay" (1995): "The essay offers the most democratic access to the enduring pleasures of reading and writing literature. In this sense, the operative assumption of many, if not most, instructors at the beginning of most first-year

college composition is that anyone can write an essay" (19). While McQuade makes the point that "it is precisely because anyone can read or write an essay that the form has lost its status as a privileged literary genre," he is quick to point out what he perceives as a benefit, namely that the "essay is also the most egalitarian form of literature because it admits the broadest range of subject matter, structure, and readership" (19). I would agree with the spirit of McQuade's argument but not the substance, only because poetry, drama, and fiction, like the essay, vary in accessibility.

8. In this, I come closest to others who have argued for the "pleasure" associated with the belletristic essay and creative nonfiction (see, for instance, Brodkey [1994], Johnson [2003], and Malinowitz [2003]).

9. See James Wolcott's "Me, Myself, and I."

Appendix

Nonfiction Journals

Creative Nonfiction (www.creativenonfiction.org)
Creative Nonfiction Foundation
5501 Walnut Street, Suite 202
Pittsburgh, PA 15232

Brevity: A Journal of Concise Literary Nonfiction (www.creativenonfiction.org/brevity)
dinty@creativenonfiction.org

Fourth Genre: Explorations in Nonfiction (www.msupress.msu.edu/FourthGenre)
Department of ATL
229 Bessey Hall
Michigan State University
East Lansing, MI 48824

River Teeth: A Journal of Nonfiction Narrative (www.ashland.edu/colleges/arts_sci/english/riverteeth)
Department of English
Ashland University
Ashland, OH 44805

Works Cited

Anderson, Chris, ed. 1989. *Literary Nonfiction: Theory, Criticism, Pedagogy.* Carbondale: Southern Illinois University Press.

Atkins, G. Douglas. 2000. "Art and Anger—Upon Taking Up the Pen Again: On Self(e)-Expression." *JAC* 20 (2): 414-26.

———. 2000. "On Writing Well; Or, Spring the Genie from the Inkpot: A Not-So-Modest Proposal." *JAC* 20 (1): 73-85.

Atwan, Robert. 1995. "The Essay—Is It Literature?" In Forman 1995, 21–37.

Bakhtin, M. M. 1990. *Art and Answerability: Early Philosophical Essays.* Ed. Michael Holquist and Vadim Liapunov, trans. Vadim Liapunov. Austin: University of Texas Press.

Barrie, J. M. 1902. *The Little White Bird; Or, Adventures in Kensington Gardens.* New York: C. Scribner's Sons.

———. 1906; repr. 1991. *Peter Pan in Kensington Gardens.* Oxford: Oxford University Press.

———. 1911; repr. 1991. *Peter and Wendy.* Oxford: Oxford University Press.

Baym, Nina. 1998. "Women's Novels and Women's Minds: An Unsentimental View of Nineteenth-Century American Women's Fiction." *Novel* 31: 335–350.

Bishop, Wendy. 1997. *Teaching Lives: Essays and Stories.* Logan: Utah State University Press.

Bizzell, Patricia. 1999. "Hybrid Academic Discourses: What, Why, How." *Composition Studies* 27 (2): 7–22.

———. 2000. "Basic Writing and the Issue of Correctness; or, What to Do with 'Mixed' Forms of Academic Discourse." *Journal of Basic Writing* 19 (1): 4–12.

Bloom, Lynn Z. 1998. *Composition Studies as a Creative Art.* Logan: Utah State University Press.

Boetcher Joeres, Ruth-Ellen and Elizabeth Mittman, ed. 1993. *The Politics of the Essay: Feminist Perspectives.* Bloomington, IN: Indiana University Press.

Brodkey, Linda. 1994. "Writing on the Bias." *College English* 56: 527–47.

Brueggemann, Brenda Jo. 2002. *Lend Me Your Ear: Rhetorical Constructions of Deafness.* Washington, D.C.: Gallaudet University Press.

Butrym, Alexander J., ed. 1989. *Essays on the Essay: Redefining the Genre.* Athens, GA: University of Georgia Press.

Chevalier, Tracy, ed. 1997. *The Encyclopedia of the Essay.* London: Fitzroy Dearborn.

Clark, Suzanne. 1991. *Sentimental Modernism: Women Writers and the Revolution of the Word.* Bloomington: Indiana University Press.

———. 1994. "Rhetoric, Social Construction, and Gender: Is It Bad to Be Sentimental?" In *Writing Theory and Critical Theory,* ed. John Clifford and John Schilb, 96–108. Research and Scholarship in Composition 3. New York: Modern Language Association.

Corey, Mary F. 1999. *The World through a Monocle:* The New Yorker *at Midcentury.* Cambridge, MA: Harvard University Press.

Cushman, Ellen. 2001. "The Politics of the Personal: Storying Our Lives against the Grain." *College English* 64: 41–62.

Davis, Linda H. 1989. *Onward and Upward: A Biography of Katharine S. White.* New York: Fromm International.

de Obaldia, Claire. 1995. *The Essayistic Spirit.* Oxford.

Dennis, Patrick. 1955; repr. 2001. *Auntie Mame: An Irreverent Escapade.* New York: Broadway Books.

Elbow, Peter. 1990. "Forward: About Personal Expressive Writing." *Pre/Text* 11 (1–2): 7–20.

———. 2000. *Everyone Can Write: Essays Toward a Hopeful Theory of Writing and Teaching Writing.* New York: Oxford University Press.

Eldred, Janet Carey. 1988/1989. "Faulkner's Still Life: Art and Abortion in *The Wild Palms.*" *The Faulkner Journal* 4 (1–2): 139–58.

Elledge, Scott. 1984. *E. B. White: A Biography.* New York: Norton.

Fakundiny, Lydia. 1990. *The Art of the Essay.* Boston: Houghton Mifflin.

Faulkner, William. 1936; repr. 1972. *Absalom, Absalom!* New York: Vintage.

———. 1939; repr. *The Wild Palms.* New York: Vintage, 1966.

Flower, Linda S. and John R. Hayes. 1981. "A Cognitive Process Theory of Writing." *CCC* 32: 365–87.

Forché, Carolyn and Philip Gerard. *Writing Creative Nonfiction.* Cincinnati: Story Press, 2001.

Forman, Janis, ed. 1995. *What Do I Know? Reading, Writing, and Teaching the Essay.* Portsmouth, NH: Boynton/Cook.

Gere, Anne Ruggles. 2001. "The Politics of the Personal: Storying Our Lives against the Grain." *College English* 64: 41–62.

Gere, Anne Ruggles and Cynthia Margaret Gere. 1998. "Living with Fetal Alcohol Syndrome/Fetal Alcohol Effect (FAS/FAE)." *Michigan Quarterly Review* 37 (3). www.umich.edu/~mqr

Gill, Brendan. 1975; repr. 1997. *Here at* The New Yorker. New York: Da Capo Press.

Gilman, Charlotte Perkins. 1892; repr. 1998. *The Yellow Wall-Paper.* Ed. Dale M. Bauer. Boston: Bedford (Bedford Cultural Editions).

Gilyard, Keith. (1991). *Voices of the Self.* Detroit: Wayne State University Press.

Goldthwaite, Melissa. 2003. "Confessionals." *College English* 66: 55–73.

Good, Graham. 1988. *The Observing Self: Rediscovering the Essay.* London: Routledge.

Gopnik, Adam. 2000. *Paris to the Moon.* New York: Random House.

Grant, Jane. 1968. *Ross,* The New Yorker, *and Me.* New York: Reynal.

Gray, Paul. 1996. "Winfrey's Winners: Oprah Recommends a Book on TV and—Bingo!—Her Viewers Turn It into an Instant Best Seller." *Time,* Dec. 2, 84.

Haswell, Richard H. and Min-Zhan Lu. 2000. *Comp Tales. An Introduction to College Composition through its Stories.* New York: Longman.

Hawisher, Gail E., and Cynthia L. Selfe, eds. 1999. *Passions, Pedagogies, and 21st Century Technologies.* Logan: Utah State University Press.

Heilker, Paul. 1996. *The Essay: Theory and Pedagogy for an Active Form.* Urbana, IL: National Council of Teachers of English.

Hesse, Douglass. 1991. "The Recent Rise of Literary Nonfiction: A Cautionary Assay." *JAC* 11 (2): 323–34.

Holdstein, Deborah H. and David Bleich, eds. 2001. *Personal Effects: The Social Character of Scholarly Writing.* Logan UT: Utah State University Press.

Hope International. 2000. "Adoption Project Proposal." http://www.hopeintl.org/adoption.htm.

Johnson, T. R. 2003. *A Rhetoric of Pleasure: Prose Style and Today's Composition Classroom.* Cross Currents: New Perspectives in Rhetoric and Composition. Portsmouth, NH: Boynton/Cook.

Kameen, Paul. 1999. "Re-covering Self in Composition." *College English* 62: 100–111.

Kamler, Barbara. 2001. *Relocating the Personal: A Critical Writing Pedagogy.* Albany: State University of New York Press.

Kincaid, Jamaica. 1997. Afterword to *Onward and Upward in the Garden*, by Katharine S. White, ed. E. B. White. New York: North Point.

Kirklighter, Cristina. 2002. *Traversing the Democratic Borders of the Essay.* Albany: State University of New York Press.

Kirsch, Gesa. 2001. "The Politics of the Personal: Storying Our Lives against the Grain." *College English* 64: 41–62.

Klaus, Carl H. 1995. "Excursions of the Mind: Toward a Poetics of Uncertainty in the Disjunctive Essay." In Forman 1995, 39–53.

Kunkel, Thomas. 1995. *Genius in Disguise.* New York: Carroll and Graf Publishers.

Kunkel, Thomas, ed. 2000. *Letters from the Editor:* The New Yorker's *Harold Ross.* New York: The Modern Library.

Lakoff, George, and Mark Johnson. 1980. *Metaphors We Live By.* Chicago: University of Chicago Press.

Lane, Anthony. 2003. "The Fighter: Rereading Robert Lowell." *New Yorker*, June 9, 80–89.

Lauer, Janice M. 1984. "Composition Studies: Dappled Discipline." *Rhetoric Review* 3 (1): 20–29.

Lopate, Phillip. 1995. Introd. to *The Art of the Personal Essay: An Anthology from the Classical Era to the Present.* New York: Anchor.

———. 2001. "Writing Personal Essays." In *Writing Creative Nonfiction: Instruction and Insights from Teachers of the Associated Writing Programs*, ed. Carolyn Forché and Philip Gerard, 38–44. Cincinnati: Story Press.

Lu, Min-Zhan. 2001. *Shanghai Quartet: The Crossings of Four Women of China.* Emerging Writers in Creative Nonfiction Series. Pittsburgh: Duquesne University Press.

Lu, Min-Zhan, and Bruce Horner. 1998. "The Problematic of Experience: Redefining Critical Work in Ethnography and Pedagogy." *College English* 60: 257–77.

McHenry, Elizabeth. 2002. *Forgotten Readers: Recovering the Lost History of African American Literacy Societies.* Durham, NC: Duke University Press.

Malinowitz, Harriet. 1996. "David and Me." *JAC* 16 (2): 209–23.

———. 2002. "Unmotherhood." *JAC* 22 (1): 11–36.

———. 2003. "Business, Pleasure, and the Personal Essay." *College English* 65: 305–22.

Mason, Bobbie Anne. 2000. "Fallout: Paducah's Secret Nuclear Disaster." *New Yorker*, Jan. 10, 30+.

McComiskey, Bruce. 2002. Review of *Literacy Matters: Writing and Reading the Social Self*, by Robert P. Yagelski. *College Composition and Communication* 53(4): 751–54.

McHenry, Elizabeth. 2002. *Forgotten Readers: Recovering the Lost History of African American Literary Societies*. Durham, NC: Duke University Press.

McQuade, Donald. 1995. "(Re)Placing the Essay." In Forman 1995, 11–20.

Miller, Susan. 1990. "Comment on 'A Common Ground: The Essay in Academe,'" *College English* 52: 330–34.

New Yorker. 2000. Seventy-fifth anniversary special issue. Feb. 21/28.

Porter, Katherine Anne. 1990. *Letters of Katherine Anne Porter*, ed. Isabel Bayley. New York: Atlantic Monthly Press.

Publishers Weekly. 1998. "Oprah's Tender Takeover of Trade Paperbacks." Mar. 23, 56.

Recchio, Thomas E. 1994. "On the Critical Necessity of 'Essaying' V. Narrating the Writing Process." In *Taking Stock: The Writing Process Movement in the 90s*, ed. Lad Tobin and Thomas Newkirk, 219–235. Portsmouth, NH: Boynton/Cook.

Root, Robert and Michael Steinberg. 1996. *Those Who Do, Can: Teachers Writing, Writers Teaching: A Sourcebook*. Urbana IL: NCTE.

Rose, Jacqueline. 1984; repr. 1993. *The Case of Peter Pan, or The Impossibility of Children's Fiction*. Philadelphia: University of Pennsylvania Press.

Rose, Mike. 1990. *Lives on the Boundary*. New York: Penguin.

Ross, Lillian. 1998. *Here but Not Here: A Love Story (My Life with William Shawn and* The New Yorker*)*. New York: Random House.

Schroeder, Christopher, Helen Fox, and Patricia Bizzell, eds. 2003. *Alt Dis: Alternative Discourses and the Academy*. Portsmouth, NH: Boynton/Cook.

Seebohm, Caroline. 1982. *The Man Who Was Vogue: The Life and Times of Condé Nast*. New York: Viking.

Selfe, Cynthia. 2000. "To His Nibs, G. Douglas Atkins—Just in Case You're Serious about Your Not-So-Modest Proposal." *JAC* 20 (2): 405–13.

Sommers, Nancy. 1992. "Between the Drafts." *College Composition and Communication* 43: 23–31.

———. 1993. "The Language of Coats." College English 55 (3): 420–28.

Spellmeyer, Kurt. 1993. *Common Ground: Dialogue, Understanding, and the Teaching of Composition*. Englewood Cliffs, NJ: Prentice Hall.

———. 1996. "Out of the Fashion Industry: From Cultural Studies to the Anthropology of Knowledge." *College Composition and Communication* 47: 424-36.

Strunk Jr., William. 1918. *The Elements of Style*. Ithaca, NY: priv. print. www.bartleby.com.

Tenney, Tabitha Gilman. 1801; repr. 1992. *Female Quixotism*. New York: Oxford University Press.

Thurber, James. 1959. *The Years with Ross*. Boston: Little, Brown.

Trimmer, Joseph F. ed. 1997. *Narration as Knowledge: Tales of the Teaching Life*. Portsmouth, NH: Boynton/Cook.

Villanueva, Victor. 1993. *Bootstraps: From an American Academic of Color*. Urbana, IL: National Council of Teachers of English.

Wasserstein, Wendy. 2000. "Complications." *New Yorker*, Feb. 21/28, 87+.

Welsch, Susan. 1995. "Writing: In and With the World." *College Composition and Communication* 46: 103–7.

White, E. B. 1976. *Letters of E. B. White*. Ed. Dorothy Lobrano Guth. New York: Harper Colophon.

Wilson, Emily Herring, ed. 2002. *Two Gardeners: Katharine S. White and Elizabeth Lawrence—A Friendship in Letters*. Boston: Beacon.

Wolcott, James. 1997. "Me, Myself, and I." *Vanity Fair*. October, 212+.

Wolfe, Tom. 2000. *Hooking Up*. New York : Farrar, Straus, and Giroux.

Yagoda, Ben. 2000. *About Town.* The New Yorker *and the World It Made.* New York: Scribner.